DON'T E...
How to stop blaming ...

TONY GOUGH was born in London in 1931. After working as an accountant, and National Service in the Royal Air Force, he trained for ordination in the Church of England. He served in pastoral ministry for twenty years before leaving for post-graduate work in the United States. He holds the Diploma in Theology from London University, a Master's degree from the University of Leicester, and a Doctor of Ministry degree in pastoral psychology from the Chicago Theological Seminary where he graduated (with distinction) in 1981. Since then he has been in private practice as a psychotherapist and counsellor. His first two books, *Couples Arguing* (DLT, 1987) and *Couples in Counselling* (DLT, 1989), have been widely acclaimed as breaking new ground in the areas of human communication skills and the understanding of the counselling process.

Overcoming Common Problems Series

Overcoming Common Problems Series

Feverfew
A traditional herbal remedy for migraine
and arthritis
DR STEWART JOHNSON

Fight Your Phobia and Win
DAVID LEWIS

Getting Along with People
DIANNE DOUBTFIRE

Goodbye Backache
DR DAVID IMRIE WITH COLLEEN
DIMSON

Helping Children Cope with Divorce
ROSEMARY WELLS

Helping Children Cope with Grief
ROSEMARY WELLS

How to be a Successful Secretary
SUE DYSON AND STEPHEN HOARE

How to Be Your Own Best Friend
DR PAUL HAUCK

How to Control your Drinking
DRS W. MILLER AND R. MUNOZ

How to Cope with Stress
DR PETER TYRER

**How to Cope with Tinnitus and Hearing
Loss**
DR ROBERT YOUNGSON

How to Cope with Your Child's Allergies
DR PAUL CARSON

How to Cure Your Ulcer
ANNE CHARLISH AND DR BRIAN
GAZZARD

How to Do What You Want to Do
DR PAUL HAUCK

How to Enjoy Your Old Age
DR B. F. SKINNER AND M. E.
VAUGHAN

How to Get Things Done
ALISON HARDINGHAM

How to Improve Your Confidence
DR KENNETH HAMBLY

How to Interview and Be Interviewed
MICHELE BROWN AND GYLES
BRANDRETH

How to Love a Difficult Man
NANCY GOOD

How to Love and be Loved
DR PAUL HAUCK

How to Make Successful Decisions
ALISON HARDINGHAM

How to Move House Successfully
ANNE CHARLISH

How to Pass Your Driving Test
DONALD RIDLAND

How to Say No to Alcohol
KEITH McNEILL

How to Spot Your Child's Potential
CECILE DROUIN AND ALAIN DUBOS

How to Stand up for Yourself
DR PAUL HAUCK

**How to Start a Conversation and Make
Friends**
DON GABOR

How to Stop Feeling Guilty
DR VERNON COLEMAN

How to Stop Smoking
GEORGE TARGET

How to Stop Taking Tranquillisers
DR PETER TYRER

How to Stop Worrying
DR FRANK TALLIS

Hysterectomy
SUZIE HAYMAN

If Your Child is Diabetic
JOANNE ELLIOTT

Jealousy
DR PAUL HAUCK

Learning to Live with Multiple Sclerosis
DR ROBERT POVEY, ROBIN DOWIE
AND GILLIAN PRETT

Overcoming Common Problems Series

Overcoming Common Problems

DON'T BLAME ME!

How to stop blaming yourself and other people

Tony Gough

SHELDON PRESS
LONDON

First published in Great Britain 1990
Sheldon Press, SPCK, Marylebone Road, London NW1 4DU

We are grateful to the following for permission to reproduce
copyright material: John Cleese and Connie Booth for the
extract from *The Complete Fawlty Towers* (pp.14–15);
Jules Feiffer and Shanks, Davis and Remer for the cartoon
which first appeared in the *Observer*, 20 February 1977
(p.25).

British Library Cataloguing in Publication Data

Gough, Tony
    Don't blame me!: how to stop blaming yourself and other people.
    I. Title
    158.1

    ISBN 0–85969–609–X

Typeset by Deltatype Ltd, Ellesmere Port.
Printed in Great Britain by Courier International Ltd, Tiptree, Essex

Contents

Acknowledgements

I gladly acknowledge my debt to the writings of Dr Eric Berne and his concepts of Transactional Analysis outlined in *Games People Play*. Interestingly enough, he never mentions The Blaming Game either in his list of 'games' or in the index of that book. However, the *issue* of blaming is implicit in many games that he describes, and I am happy to acknowledge how much I owe to the principles and practice of TA in my work.

I am also grateful to Dr Marilyn Aitkenhead for assistance in my research into the psychological theory of attribution in human behaviour. I valued her interest and encouragement.

I would like to thank the Senior Editor of Sheldon Press, Joanna Moriarty, for her enthusiastic support of this book, especially in its first draft. She made some important suggestions as to its future shape, and I am grateful for her insights. The remaining blemishes are, of course, my own.

Introduction

A man was walking along a river bank when he heard cries for help coming from someone in the river. He dived in at once and brought the drowning woman to the river bank and applied mouth-to-mouth resuscitation. As she revived, the man was astonished to hear further cries for help from a man in distress. He, too, was saved and brought to the safety of the river bank and the care of the crowd which had gathered to watch this act of bravery. Even as he climbed out of the river, there were further urgent cries for help coming from the middle of the river. The man said to the crowd, 'You go and rescue this one; I'm off upstream to find out who's pushing all these people into the water!'

This story (told in Gerard Egan, *The Skilled Helper*, Brooks/ Cole 1982, p. 301) describes why this book came to be written. The old proverb reminds us that prevention is better than cure, and while the rescuer in the story was doing a brave thing he also became curious, as a result of his work, as to how all these people were getting themselves into the river in the first place. There are, of course, many people who in these days of job descriptions would simply stick to their own job and not bother their heads about things they consider to be none of their business. A full-time lifeguard might be doing a marvellous job in saving people's lives, but never wonder about the cause of their distress, when in fact, further along the beach, there is a boat hire firm letting out a fleet of rotting dinghies through which most of the people he is rescuing have fallen! Where does responsibility lie?

Perhaps a psychotherapist, who is also a writer, asks this sort of question. As a therapist, I spend most of my life 'patching up' people in distress; but as a writer, I take time out from my work as a 'paramedic' at the foot of the cliff, and climb up to find out who's pushing all these people through the fence at the top of the cliff!

1

I firmly believe that there is a huge hole in the fence, marked 'The Blaming Game: push here!' So many of the people I counsel are suffering from the long-term effects of other people's blame: they have been 'scapegoated', often for as long as they can remember, and this has eaten away almost every vestige of self-respect and self-esteem. Many of them are broken, and on the edge of despair and just giving up. While there will always be a need for trained counsellors to listen and respond to their situations (the world is never going to be perfect), I want to complement my work as therapist by drawing attention to the need for more therapeutic models of human behaviour to prevent much of this unnecessary pain and affliction.

One instance comes to mind: it concerns the story of an American, Donnie Moore, aged 35, who was a star pitcher with the California Angels baseball team. The Angels were just one strike away from the World Series – like getting to the finals of the F.A. Cup – when Moore, pitching with an injured shoulder, threw a pitch that was hit out of the ground, and cost The Angels the match. A friend of his said, 'He was never himself again; that home run killed him. He blamed himself for the Angels not going to the World Series.' Donnie Moore subsequently shot and killed himself.

'Exceptional', you say. 'The man was clearly out of his mind.' Of course, you might be right: we'll never know. But it illustrates the deadly power of self-blame, and where it can lead, without diagnosis and treatment. Each of us could, without a great deal of thought, share incidents in which we were accused unfairly or where we simply took on board far more responsibility than we need have done. In either case, the rules of the 'blaming game' are at work. Or, perhaps much more frequently, we actually blame other people in an attempt to excuse ourselves or get ourselves off the hook. Blaming is so common that its deadly effects often get overlooked.

I hope that this book can begin to get the effects of blaming back on to the agenda of human behaviour and consider some therapeutic alternatives to its sinister and destructive work. In the process, we may discover some uncomfortable truths about ourselves; self-examination carries its own cost as well as its own reward.

In an age where 'green' issues have come to the top of the national and international agenda, and pollution from all sources is receiving stringent and searching examination, together with strategies for improvement, perhaps this small book could be thought of as a 'green book' for human relationships, a book which helps remove some of the toxic effects of blame which poison and destroy our inner landscape and rob it of its much-needed beauty and power.

Tony Gough
Western Park
Leicester

1

What is 'The Blaming Game'?

Blaming is universal. Its practice is endemic in the human race, and covers every race and social grouping. It has gone on from time immemorial in one form or another. It is even older than the oldest profession! Our mythical parents, Adam and Eve, were busy passing the buck (or was it the apple?) right at the beginning of the human story in the Garden of Eden; the man blamed the woman, and the woman blamed the snake. Commenting on this primal scene, C. R. Snyder writes: 'the first free act of humankind . . . was not accompanied with a sense of pride and accomplishment but, rather, with an excuse.' (*Excuses,* John Wiley & Sons 1983, p. 9) 'The blaming game' was thus the very first game that people played.

Like other games people play, the blaming game is governed by certain rules. Considering how long blaming has been around, you would think that we might have got the hang of these rules by now. But have we? We have all had the experience of being on the receiving end of unfair blaming. Does this mean that blaming is 'a bad thing'? Some people we know seem to have turned fault-finding into an art form; they are past-masters at blamesmanship. So is its use *ever* warranted? How can we tell when blaming is deserved or not? Many questions arise on this important yet elusive subject and I shall be examining some of them in this book. By way of introduction I would like you to consider this story.

Case history: Tom and Betty

Tom and Betty had been married for ten years; they had one child. One day Tom confessed to Betty that he had been having an affair with his secretary at work. For a while he continued to live at home, but eventually the situation deteriorated between them, and Tom decided to leave.

Several days later Betty put the child in the car, and drove it over a cliff; both of them were killed.

Who would you say was to blame for this tragedy? Was it:

- the husband, for having the affair which affected the wife?
- the other woman, for having an affair with a married man?
- Betty, for killing herself and their child?

Some people would see this as an open-and-shut case. Tom, of course, must bear full responsibility for the tragedy. If he had not been unfaithful in the first place, it would never have happened. End of story.

But such a simplistic (albeit understandable) view leaves some rather uncomfortable questions unanswered, including where the distinction lies between moral and legal responsibility. It also leaves out the issue of the *degree* of responsibility that Betty must bear for her own actions. No one made her drive her car over the cliff; in fact, there were several options that lay to hand:

1. She could have put up with the separation and sought to make a new life for herself and their child.
2. She could have killed the mistress.
3. She could have killed Tom.
4. She could have just killed herself, and not the child as well.

So placing all the blame on Tom does not do justice to the facts. Just suppose that Betty had survived the suicide attempt, we can imagine some of the excuses she might have made to her rescuers:

My husband drove me to it!

(*Response*: Untrue. Betty drove the car, not Tom. Even had he made the suggestion, told her to do it, showed her the nearest cliff on the map, and given her car a push start, he was still not responsible for the deaths. Quite literally, Betty 'drove' herself to it!)

It was all that other woman's fault!

(*Response:* Untrue. As in all affairs, this begs the question of the quality of the marriage for which Betty, in part, was responsible.)

These possible reactions by Betty are both statements that reflect an abdication of responsibility; and, as in every case when this happens, blaming must be employed to fill the gap left by our lack of integrity.

Blame, therefore, is what is left when we abdicate personal responsibility.

We can see in the story of Tom and Betty what happens when we attempt an easy solution to a complex issue. For us to blame Tom entirely for the deaths of his wife and child would be grossly unfair. But suppose, for the purpose of illustration, Tom were to play the same blaming game and take full responsibility for what happened? What if he were to develop an unmanageable guilt complex and seek therapeutic help? What would Tom need to become aware of?

First, Tom needs to recognize that he did not kill his wife and child. He may, however, need to reach down deep in his feelings, and discover how he feels towards his wife for killing an innocent child. My guess would be that underneath his grief lies an enormous amount of anger towards Betty for what she did. Most suicides include 'targeting' an individual or a group of individuals (consciously or not) who would be most affected by the death, and in this case it is easy to spot that both Tom and his mistress have been 'set up' by Betty to pick up the pieces.

Second, Tom needs to avoid turning the blame inwards towards himself. He should accept the part that his affair played in his wife's decision to kill herself, while *not* taking responsibility for her decision to do so.

Third, Tom needs to express his feelings about what has happened, both his grief, especially for his child, and his anger towards Betty. Expressing anger towards the dead is never an easy thing to do, given the cultural taboos concerning 'speaking ill of the dead'. But such superstitious nonsense belongs to a previous age when we lived in fear of being haunted by the dead.

Fourth, Tom needs to be able to live out his life creatively, free from the guilt of the past. This is not simply a case of 'forgive and forget'; such tragedies are not easily forgotten. But he would need to forgive himself for his part in contributing to the circumstances surrounding the tragedy. He is, of course, responsible for the affair – but *not* for the deaths.

In reality, life's circumstances can be even more complicated than this somewhat simplistic story has indicated. Supposing, for instance, that Betty was suffering from premenstrual tension, and her GP had refused to prescribe any medication? Would *he* be to blame? Or, had her mother rung up that morning to say she was worried about father who had had a relapse in hospital, was she to blame for causing further worry? In our desire for 'causes' of events, we can get pushed into all kinds of areas with no 'final cause' at all, just a mass of circumstantial evidence. If three people, for example, each held different views about who was to blame for this particular tragedy there is no way of deciding who is right. Each of the three has an element of truth, but no-one could possibly adjudicate upon a final and definitive culprit to the crime. We would just have to agree to differ.

Apportioning blame

It is this difficulty in apportioning blame that causes so many arguments and much bitterness in human relationships.

Consider another situation: A plane crashes; whose fault is it?

1. Is it metal fatigue, the fault of the manufacturers?
2. Is it the fault of the mechanic who checked the plane but failed to notice the cracks?
3. Is it the pilot's fault? Did he make a fatal error?
4. Is it the punishing schedule of the airline directors who do not put enough capital into maintaining their aircraft or supplying new ones?

5. Is it the fault of the holidaymakers who want cheap package holidays?
6. Is it a terrorist bomb?

We finally discover that it was a bomb, placed in the luggage compartment by a terrorist. Other questions now arise:

1. How was the bomb placed on board: a passenger? an airport worker? a switch of suitcases?
2. What organization planted the bomb?
3. Who, within that organization, ordered the sabotage?
4. What grievance does this organization have against the airline or passengers who use it?
5. What political motives are involved?
6. Had the airline refused to pay a ransom?
7. Was security at the airport lax?
8. How far is the Minister of Transport to blame for not responding to calls for extra security at airports?
9. How far is the taxpayer to blame for wanting reduced income tax?

We could go on for ever finding a cause for every effect as we search for our culprit who must bear the blame for the bombed plane. But loose ends abound in life: even after we ascertain the cause of a plane crash, this merely serves to open up a host of subsidiary questions, and the arguments seem to go on for ever. Every national and international tragedy over the past few years bears witness to this phenomenon. On some occasions there is a refreshingly honest confession of fault, like a car driver who admits to an error of human judgement due to overwork. More often, however, there is nothing but denial and evasion.

When we try to apportion blame, is it just an insatiable curiosity or a more worthy attitude such as seeing justice done? Have we some righteous need to see that the guilty are punished? However we understand it, blaming is certainly motivated by some human need to make sense of the world in which we live, to deliver us from living in a world of madness and chance; blaming establishes some semblance of sense and order, a rational framework within which we can live our lives.

Blaming then, is our attempt to establish order out of chaos. So far, so good.

Responsibility

However complex some human situations can be, it is often appropriate to respond to that need within us to attribute causes to effects. If that means accusing people of doing wrong, so be it. There is, therefore, an appropriate use of blame in human affairs. For blame is always linked to another important concept, that of *responsibility*.

The illustrations above all contain a degree of responsibility. Betty, who drove herself and her child off the edge of the cliff, has to bear some degree of responsibility for her actions. Likewise, Tom and his mistress share some responsibility for the creation of the affair against which Betty reacted so violently. It is here that we need to note an important element in our understanding of blaming: blaming is not always 'either/or'; it is seldom a question of two extremes – right or wrong – blaming is better seen and understood as a *continuum* with gradations of blame as 'more-or-less' (Fig. 1). Blaming has to do with *degrees* of responsibility, rather than an 'all-or-nothing' attitude. While there will always be cases where guilt or innocence is apparent and indisputable, and any blame is either accepted or attributed without question, there are always cases, perhaps the majority, where no such 'either/or' is possible.

So, in Betty's case we could say that responsibility could and maybe should be shared by all three adults, the child remaining an unwitting victim. Tom is responsible for the affair, and for breaking up the marriage. The 'other woman' is responsible for her part in the affair. The wife is responsible for her choices and for the ultimate death of their child. Seen from this vantage point, blame is something that is shared around, rather than dumped on one person. Of course, this is not an exact science; we can never get to the point of saying just how much blame each

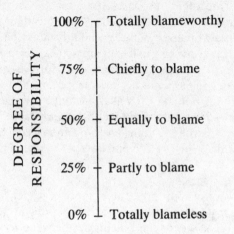

Fig. 1 The continuum of blame

should take, in a mathematical sense. But seen as a continuum, we are able to make sense of the story, and we are delivered from simplistic 'black-and-white' responses which do less than justice to what is, after all, a very complicated scenario.

When is blaming appropriate?

We have looked briefly at the way in which blaming works in human relationships, and we can now see that there is a strong case to make out for the *appropriateness* of such an activity. Some people are of the opinion that, as one man said to me recently, 'Blaming is a word that should be expunged from the dictionary!' There is nothing wrong with appropriately attributing causes to actions. On occasions I will need to say, however hard it might be for me to do so, 'This is my fault. I am responsible for that.' Equally, there will be occasions when I will need to say, 'This is *your* fault. I am not responsible for that.' These two reactions represent 'healthy' responses to factors for which I am, and am not, responsible.

11

But there are other responses, traditionally associated with human behaviour, that are 'unhealthy', the untruthful statements that either accuse others or ourselves unfairly. Some people blame other people for everything that happens to them, even when this is manifestly untrue; others blame themselves for everything, even when they are obviously not responsible. So one attitude accepts responsibility for nothing ('It's all your fault!'), while the other accepts responsibility for everything ('It's all my fault!').

There are, therefore, four basic positions concerning the nature of blame, which we can illustrate as shown in Figs 2 and 3.

Confession

Figure 2a shows an appropriate acceptance of responsibility, and contains the truth about me and the truth about you. I am guilty, you are not. This keeps the boundaries between us clear, and allows me to deal with the situation free from blaming others for what I have done. I do this by confession of what I have done to whoever it affects.

Denial

Figure 2b shows what happens in an unhealthy response. Although I am in fact guilty, I resort to blaming instead. So I distort the truth both about you ('It's your fault!') and about me ('It's not my fault!'). This is an inappropriate attribution of responsibility and the method I use is denial.

Confrontation

Figure 3a shows how I respond when I am not at fault. If it is obvious to me that you are to blame, I can say so clearly. I do this by an appropriate attribution of responsibility to where blame lies (with you), and I can retain a healthy sense of my own lack of guilt, using confrontation to accomplish this.

Introjection

Figure 3b shows an unhealthy, even neurotic response to events where I bear no actual responsibility at all. I will, however, for reasons to be explained later, assume responsibility for

Fig. 2 When truth = 'I did it' | **Fig. 3** When truth = 'I didn't do it'

HEALTHY RESPONSE | HEALTHY RESPONSE

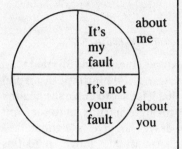 |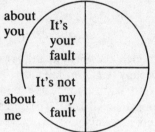

Fig. 2A = appropriate *acceptance* of responsibility
Verdict = real guilt
Method = confession

Fig. 3A = appropriate *attribution* of responsibility
Verdict = real innocence
Method = confrontation

UNHEALTHY RESPONSE | UNHEALTHY RESPONSE

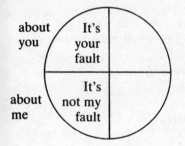 |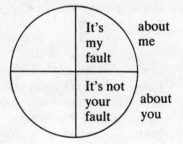

Fig. 2B = inappropriate *attribution* of responsibility
Verdict = false innocence
Method = denial and projection

Fig. 3B = inappropriate *acceptance* of responsibility
Verdict = false guilt
Method = introjection

everything that happens, even when I am not involved. I will distort the truth about you and about me, and we see this as an inappropriate acceptance of responsibility. The method used is called introjection, an absorbing into oneself of responsibility that actually lies elsewhere.

Healthy versus unhealthy responses

Although it is the unhealthy responses (Figs 2b and 3b) that tend to occupy our attention most, because of their intrinsic distortion of truth, it must not be assumed that it is easy to make the healthy responses in all cases. To confess to our own faults, or to confront others about theirs, is never easy. To give a lighthearted illustration, as distinct from the tragic one above, take this contribution from the television classic, *Fawlty Towers*. Basil Fawlty has noticed two people embracing, and not knowing they are father and daughter mistakes this for an illicit union. He tells the guests to leave, but is immediately confronted by his wife, the indomitable Sybil. The dialogue runs like this:

SYBIL: What have you done?

BASIL: I told them to leave.

SYBIL: You've told them to leave?

BASIL: Well, how was I supposed to know? Why didn't you tell me, you halfwit? Why didn't they tell me? You can't blame me for this.

SYBIL: Go and tell them they can stay.

BASIL: Why don't you go and tell them?

SYBIL: I didn't tell them to go.

BASIL: No, no, I suppose it's all my fault, isn't it?

SYBIL: Go and tell them! Now!

BASIL: No, I won't.

SYBIL: You will.

BASIL: No, I won't.

SYBIL: Oh yes you will.

BASIL: Oh yes I will. Right! That's right – leave it to me! Let me get you out of it. That's what I'm good for, isn't it? Basil

Fawlty Limited. Other people's messes cleared up. By appointment to my wife Sybil . . . I mean, what am I going to say?

SYBIL: Tell them you made a mistake.

BASIL: Oh, brilliant. Is that what made Britain great? 'I'm so sorry I made a mistake.' What have you got for a brain – spongecake? (*hurtles off upstairs, rehearsing to himself*) 'I'm so sorry I made a mistake, I'm so sorry I made a mistake. . . .'

(to the occupants of the room) I'm sorry . . . I'm so sorry, but my *wife* has made a mistake, I don't know how she did it, but she did, she's made a complete pudding of the whole thing as usual, it'll be perfectly all right for you to stay, I've sorted it all out, I'm frightfully sorry but you know what women are like, they've only got one brain between the lot of them, well not all of them but some of them have, particularly my wife, so please do stay and see you all later on, thank you so much . . . please do stay, my wife made a most dreadful mistake.

(©John Cleese and Connie Booth, *The Complete Fawlty Towers*, Methuen 1988, pp. 70–1)

We may believe that 'honesty is the best policy' but losing face by owning up to what we have done, or losing the friendship of others by confronting them about what they have done, can be a very costly enterprise, especially for the Basil Fawltys of this world. After all, we may upset someone!

In the uncanny way that my counselling and my writing coincide (Carl Jung referred to it as 'synchronicity'), I had just reached this point when a man arrived to see me for the first time. He felt depressed and was recommended to see me by his boss. It transpired that he had been involved in an accident that resulted in the deaths of two children. I admired the man's honesty as he wrestled with the situation in which he found himself. In his head he knew that, to some degree at least, he was responsible; but what he could not believe was how he could have done such a thing! One moment he 'couldn't believe I could have done it',

15

and the next he considered himself to be 'a murderer'. Using our model, he was wobbling (quite naturally) between the healthy response shown in Fig. 2a and the unhealthy one in Fig. 3b. Psychologically, he was wrestling painfully with his loss of self-image. He happened to be a very loving father to his own children, and the thought of killing innocent children was totally abhorrent to him. He faced his appropriate 'self-blame' with total honesty; but the long-term implications of that honesty will take some while to sink in so that a new self-image, incorporating both the fact and the future possibility of error, can emerge. In this case there was no question of culpable guilt, and the inquest found the cause of death as 'accidental'.

Denying responsibility

At this point, it may be useful to check out our own awareness concerning our human potential for error and wrongdoing. Using the continuum of our readiness to accept appropriate blame, where would you place yourself on this scale as a general habit? (Circle one)

'When I do wrong, I am prepared to accept the blame. . . .'

Almost always	Most of the time	Very often	Often	Occasionally	Rarely	Never
7	6	5	4	3	2	1

Perhaps you can discover for yourself what your personal responsibility quotient is from this scale; 3 and below will indicate your tendency to blame other people instead. So if you are one of the '3 and unders', try another test of your awareness. Complete this sentence:

'I am unready to accept blame, even when I am in the wrong, because......................'

Somewhere in your answer it is likely that you will find an emotion or a consequence by which you are threatened, or a

16

reaction by others that would be hard to cope with. As this is a self-help book, try helping yourself to discover the origins of the reactions by which you usually deny responsibility. Somewhere in your past, experience has taught you to deny that for which you are in fact responsible.

False innocence and false guilt

This brings us to the other half of our model, the two inappropriate responses to what happens to and around us, as shown in Figs 2b and 3b.

These represent two extremes of unhealthy responses. We have experienced them many times in other people, but are we sufficiently aware of our own inclinations to use them? We are talking, first, about people who deny they are ever responsible, when it is obvious to a blind rabbit with migraine that they are; and, second, about people who accept responsibility for everything that happens to them or others, when in fact they are innocent of any such thing. These are the twin faces of false innocence, and false guilt.

False innocence, taking responsibility for nothing, and false guilt, taking responsibility for everything are at opposite ends of the continuum of blame. There are serious personality deficiencies in the person who is chronically unable to accept appropriate responsibility for his/her own actions. We shall look at the origins of such behaviour in Chapter 2, but suffice it to say at this point that there is always a 'logic' even to the most bizarre patterns of behaviour. Similarly, there is the person who is unable to let others take responsibility for his/her own actions, but feels compelled to accept liability. Should two people collide in the local supermarket, for example, the first person as shown in Fig. 2b would probably say, 'Why don't you look where you're going?', while the second person (see Fig. 3b) would say, 'Oh, I'm dreadfully sorry; I shouldn't be so clumsy!' These are automatic responses, a reflex action, and not the subject of careful thought; like most habits they seem to have a life of their own. Indeed, the difficulty is often that people have become so used to reacting in either of these two inappropriate ways, that they are by now no longer conscious of them. One suffers from a presumed sense of innocence, while the other suffers from a presumed sense of guilt. Both can become chronic conditions.

Naturally, serious consequences can follow from behaviour patterns in these people, especially for their families, and we shall examine the full implications in Chapter 4. At this point, however, it is important to notice that the distinctions I am outlining are not just of academic interest; they lie somewhere at the heart of much human misery and our capacity not only for the full enjoyment of life, but also of our ability to fulfil our potential as human beings.

Summary

We noticed at the beginning of this book an important distinction between the appropriate and the inappropriate use of the category of blame. Figures 2 and 3 show us how we can choose between the 'healthy' and the 'unhealthy' responses to the actions and words of ourselves and of others. The four basic positions portray these responses as affecting the truth about me and the truth about you, and how we can distort this truth into an unfair attribution of blame either to you or to me. As these themes are developed, we will enter the shadowy, grey areas of life where such neat distinctions are hard to make; but at least the model provides us with a kind of map to help us chart our way.

Since blaming is universal – hardly a day goes by without ourselves or someone around us using it, rightly or wrongly; and since it adversely affects the lives of millions of people, why do we continue to do it? Is there a rationale behind it, some human need that blaming appears to fulfil? I think there is.

2

Why Does it Happen?

Why do we blame other people?

In the beginning was the excuse.

Way back in the mists of our human evolution, it became necessary for emerging *Homo sapiens* to understand something about his environment. His very survival depended on it. So Man worked out what made things happen, cause and effect, and his answers centred on three different kinds of situations:

- things he could attribute to his own behaviour
- things he could attribute and explain only by other people's behaviour
- events due to external, environmental factors.

As an example of the first situation, let us suppose that prehistoric Man discovered that when he was hungry it was because he had not eaten, and therefore needed to do so (for survival, of course). He could take responsibility for finding his own food, warmth and shelter – and live to tell the story.

As an example of the second situation, let us suppose that the food he needed was now prepared and, while his back was turned, his meal disappeared. He could not possibly be responsible for this event (unless he was suffering from amnesia, of course) and he could only attribute its disappearance to the fact that someone had pinched it!

As an example of the third kind of situation, let us suppose that he questioned all the people in his family and they denied having anything to do with the disappearance of his food. The only conclusion left was that a strong gust of wind had blown it away into the bushes; neither he nor his family were to blame, it just happened while he was not looking. And sure enough, when he came to look in the bushes there was his lunch – or what was left of it.

But supposing he had *not* found the remains of his meal, what then? He could go on believing in the 'gust of wind' theory, but he could just as well come up with a predatory animal or a visit from the neighbourhood gods. All he knew for certain was that he had not eaten the food – so someone or something else must be responsible for its disappearance. He must be more careful next time he turned his back on cooked dinners!

If such an event were to be a one-off experience, the chances are that it would have been forgotten. But if this happened more regularly he would, quite appropriately, come up with the idea that he had an enemy (a hungry enemy). So from a *fact* (the missing meal) he has to arrive at a conclusion in order to give his universe some semblance of order and meaning: 'Someone's pinching my food!' would be a good guess. His world now makes sense once more: whenever food is missing, it means that someone has stolen it.

He then notices the rather overfed dog sleeping outside the cave, and becomes suspicious. When preparing his next meal, he keeps a wary eye on the dog. He goes back into the cave but manages to watch the dog and the dinner at the same time. Sure enough, the dog demolishes the dinner in one gulp and makes off into the bush. Man now complains to the rest of his family about the thief in their midst and, taking pity on him (after all, it's not his fault his dinners keep disappearing), they give him some of theirs.

An evil thought now takes root in his mind. If I eat my dinner, and then pretend that the dog has eaten it instead, I shall be able to get *two* dinners instead of one, because the family will not see me go hungry. Sure enough, the family fall for it, so by blaming the dog he can go on enjoying double rations. How did he not think of such an easy ruse before! Man takes a giant step forward in deception.

Blaming others wrongfully always includes some degree of self-interest

In its more developed form, it would mean that Man never had to take responsibility for anything ever again. He could always attribute the blame to either someone or something else instead. Why should *he* own up and get into trouble? It was not in his interests to do so. Then one day, back at the cave. . . .

Having to share their meagre meals with Man the rest of the family found that they were continually going short as they subsidized the results of the thieving dog. One by one, they began to tell the same story; and while eating their meals in private, and pleading the thieving dog story, they expected a portion of the meals of those who had still not caught on to the game. But one day the dinner table was bare. There was no food: 'The dog had eaten it all.' However, outside by the camp fire the dog lay dead – from starvation!

Now, how could they explain that?

Since none of them was going to own up, they had only one way to go. They could not very well blame everyone else for what they themselves had been doing, as if it was all down to external, environmental forces. But try as they may, they saw no gusts of wind or ravenous gods to account for the lack of food. The family got weaker and weaker; no one was going to give in first. One by one they began to die, until only a few were left.

Man was the first to own up. He told his story of his meal in the bush, blown there by a gust of wind, and of the original theft by the family dog. It was the family's generosity that first put the idea of deception into his mind, and he owned up to the lie.

Since it was self-interest that first made Man avoid taking responsibility for the disappearance of his food, it was now the same self-interest that made him accept responsibility for what was taking place in the family. Unless he did so, both he and his family would die out completely. Once he owned up, all the rest owned up too, and they cooked a big, communal meal by way of celebration – together!

Responsibility versus blame

Such an account of the origins of something as complex as blaming is necessarily conjectural and simplistic. Nevertheless, I hope it at least points to something crucial to our understanding, namely, that the activity of blaming developed out of a natural desire to make sense of the world in which we live. To attribute properly to other people, circumstances, or even ourselves the events which take place around us is perfectly natural, and part of the way we find order in our world. When such attributions are correct, that is they correspond to reality, we might actually never use the word 'blame' at all. We could, instead, talk about 'responsibility': I am responsible, you are responsible, this/that is responsible. But since 'blame' now circulates in our language, it is important to notice how it was used as a neutral description; it was only subsequently that blame began to be seen as 'a bad thing', when it was used as a means of getting people 'off the hook'. It is this *inappropriate* use of blame that I call the blaming game. If I take responsibility for something I have done, I am not playing games either with you or myself. I am acting as a mature adult. 'I blame myself' is often seen as a refreshingly honest admission of personal responsibility.

We shall look further into the mechanics of 'game-playing' in Chapter 5, but for now it may be useful to sum up the reasons behind our blaming of other people for our own actions:

Playing the blaming game

We play the blaming game:

- when we want to protect ourselves
- when we want to avoid pain
- in order to save face
- to keep our reputation as 'good' or 'kind' or 'perfect'
- to avoid admitting mistakes
- for fear of what might happen if we owned up
- to stop people finding out about us
- when we want to hurt other people
- when we want to humiliate other people
- in order to ruin other people's reputation
- to gain time to think
- to preserve our self-image before others
- to elicit sympathy from others

Some well-worn phrases, familiar to all of us, go with this catalogue of reasons:

1. 'It wasn't my fault!' = denial (type: defensive).
2. 'Don't blame me!' = denial (type: aggressive).
3. 'Would I do a thing like that?' = consider my reputation.
4. 'What kind of a person do you think I am?' =criticize me, if you dare!
5. 'I'm not carrying the can for that!' = I don't take responsibility.
6. 'I don't know what you're talking about.' = denial (plea of ignorance).
7. 'If the cap fits, wear it!' = best means of defence is attack.
8. 'That's just the kind of thing he/she would do!' = attack other people's reputation; defend your own!
9. 'Look what you've done!' = please don't look at me!
10. 'Now look what you've made me do!' = you're the clumsy one!
11. 'You're always blaming me!' = familiarity breeds contempt!
12. 'Why don't you pick on someone else?' = bullying is immoral!
13. 'Did I do that?' = injured innocence!

Why do we blame ourselves?

At the opposite extreme of never taking responsibility for anything lies the mistake of taking responsibility for everything. Naturally, there is a history (and a very painful one at that) lying at the root of this neurotic behaviour pattern.

We need to review the history of people like this to uncover the origins of such a lie. Remember, we are not looking at the adult ability to accept and own up to appropriate blame; we are looking at an unhealthy, neurotic behaviour pattern which assumes responsibility for everything that goes wrong.

To make this easier, let us describe a person we can take as fairly typical of this 'all-my-fault' attitude. I will call her Angie.

Case history: Angie

When Angie was little, her older brothers and sisters used to blame her for everything that went wrong. It started, of course, with some actual wrongdoing of Angie's, such as when she upset the bottle of milk on the doorstep. Then she tripped over the dog and broke her mother's bone china mug. It only took a few sighs of, 'Oh, not again, Angie!' to start up the expectations that if anything got broken, it must be Angie's fault. Being older, her brothers and sisters were not slow to exploit this expectation. They soon found cunning ways to persuade their overworked mother not to look too closely into their lies and false accusations concerning their baby sister. Angie simply got scapegoated by the family. For a long time, Angie thought her name was 'O-Angie', since her name would regularly be linked with 'Oh! Angie!', said with regret and disappointment, and very soon a 'black sheep' of the family was in the making. If cakes went missing, crockery got broken, her brother's train was smashed or her sisters' dolls had eyes pulled out, it was all Angie's fault.

At first, Angie protested her innocence, but she soon gave that up because no-one believed her. She was typified in a brilliant cartoon by Jules Feiffer (*Observer Magazine*, 20 February 1977). Beside six illustrations of a puzzled little girl, a poignant soliloquy takes place.

In this very succinct way, Jules Feiffer has gone to the heart of how a neurosis is created. This little girl, like Angie, had to come to terms with two opposing realities: her own essential goodness, and the fact that she was continually being punished for being bad. Rather than hold on to the injustice of her world and the people in it, it was easier to *give up her original belief in her own essential goodness* and accept that the treatment meted out to her by others was due to her own essential badness. Now she had found a key to making sense of her world; these bad things kept happening to her simply because she *was* bad. Consequently, when people tell her she is at fault, she believes them. Even when she knows she is not to blame, she will accept the blame

I USED TO
BELIEVE
I WAS
A GOOD
GIRL.

UNTIL I LOST
MY DOLL
AND FOUND OUT
IT WASN'T LOST,
MY BIG SISTER
STOLE IT.

AND MY MOTHER
TOLD ME SHE
WAS TAKING ME
TO THE ZOO.
ONLY IT WASN'T
THE ZOO, IT
WAS SCHOOL.

AND MY FATHER
TOLD ME HE
WAS TAKING
ME TO THE
CIRCUS, ONLY
IT WASN'T
THE CIRCUS,
IT WAS THE
DENTIST.

SO THATS HOW
I FOUND OUT
I WASN'T
GOOD.

BECAUSE IF I
WAS GOOD
WHY WOULD
ALL THESE
GOOD PEOPLE
WANT TO
PUNISH ME?

because *it is easier to make sense of the world with all its injustice than to fight for her innocence in a world where she is not believed*!

It is from this initial abdication of the battle for personal justice that much of the subsequent hopelessness arises in Angie's life. She becomes one of those people whom we call pessimists, and for good reasons. All the original optimism of early childhood has been beaten out of her, either mentally or physically. The Angies of this world take all the responsibility for the woes and wrongs of life. Their sense of personal integrity and value is almost nil. They exude guilt.

There are thousands of 'ordinary people' walking about apparently completely well, but carrying the scars of their upbringing. Behind this apparent normality, however, a different reality lurks: their early physical and mental battering has left them with an innate sense of their own badness and worthlessness.

These people are not 'mentally ill'. They have what the experts might call a 'personality disorder' in the sense that they operate out of a misinterpretation about themselves and their environment. In some families their quirks end up being regarded as 'Mum's funny ways' or 'Dad's moodiness'. A husband and wife who came to see me recently concerning their relationship were asked what they would most like to see changed in their spouse's habits. The husband was quick to say, 'I wish she'd stop apologizing for who she is!' He illustrated what he meant by reminding his wife of her habit of ringing her mother and saying, 'It's only me, Mum!' The 'only' implied unimportance, insignificance, and his wife acknowledged that she had problems with her habitual way of putting herself down. What early conditioning had produced such self-devaluation, I wondered?

Others obtain their sense of badness from family stories concerning their own birth. It is hard for some people to imagine that such stories can drastically affect the way people regard themselves but it is, in my experience, tragically true. Think of the stories of your own birth, or those of your brothers and sisters that circulate among your own family members. I would be surprised if some of you have not heard the following statements made on some occasion:

- You gave me a hard time when you were born!
- You nearly killed me getting out!
- Because of you, I couldn't have any more children!
- You were born awkward – bum first!
- I had to have stitches because of you!
- I went through hell having you!

It is impossible not to pick up the *blaming* element in all these accusing statements. Sensitive children pick them up as 'all my fault . . .', because 'mother told me so'. I have heard these family stories hundreds of times, and for children who grow up believing them when they come out in later life they sound like this:

- I gave my mother a hard time when I was born!
- I nearly killed my mother getting out!
- Because of me, mother couldn't have any more children!
- I was born awkward. Bum first, mother always said!
- Mum had to have stitches because of me!
- I put my mother through hell when she had me!

The child has now *taken responsibility* for the pain and hurt of the mother, and a fully-fledged scenario of 'It was all my fault' is in operation. Now it is perfectly obvious that the child is *never* responsible for the manner of its birth, hard and long though the labour and delivery may be. The choice of the parents to have the child in the first place is the determining factor of responsibility, not the way the child gets delivered. Parents need to be most careful when describing the circumstances of their children's birth, to ensure that no matter what happened, no blame is being attributed directly or indirectly to the child. How *can* it be the child's fault? Yet thousands of people have taken on board responsibility for their mother's pain, and they carry it around with them like a debt they can never repay. 'It's my fault' is the irrational blame which hangs around their neck like a family curse. If challenged, these people would say, 'If it weren't for me . . .' and an apology for their badness or wickedness would follow: 'If it weren't for me, mother would have had other children. . . .' 'If it weren't for me, mother would not have been put off sex for life!' 'If it weren't for me mother would have had a happier life!'

Dr Paul Tournier writes:

A man whose mother died in bringing him into the world reveals himself to us as perpetually burdened with an undefinable sense of guilt, which he projects on to all he does, constantly accusing himself of imaginary sins. He is the 'overscrupulous' type. He appears to suffer from a groundless and unconscious feeling of responsibility for the death of his mother, and it seems that this remorse must be expressed in endless self-accusations, which never succeed in effacing it.

(*The Strong and the Weak*, SCM 1974, p. 220)

These 'If it weren't for me' scenarios can paralyse the lives of children who have been subjected to them over a long period of time. They suffer from *inverted blame* which causes the 'It's all my fault' attitude to life, and gives them a sense of badness, wickedness, evil or even 'sin'.

One woman told me how she was brought up by her mother and grandmother in this way. Ordinary childish naughtiness was magnified by them to life-threatening proportions. The scenario that stayed with this woman for over 50 years was still ringing in her ears: 'You'll be the death of all of us!' She was in fact convinced that she had caused her father's death, simply because it was what she had been taught by the grown-ups around her. Their word was law, and she could never challenge it. It was easier to accept that she was thoroughly bad and toxic. Like

Angie, mentioned above, it was easier to give up her original sense of her own innocence and goodness in the face of the family belief-system which blamed the child for all of the family's ills.

I have spoken to many people who believe that they are the 'black sheep' of the family. I usually check out if this is their own firmly held belief or a story that circulates in the family. Is there any objective data which can confirm their own malevolence, or rejection of society's norms? Often there is not. 'Well,' they may say, 'that's what I was always taught, anyway.' Such people appear to carry responsibility for all the family's ills on their shoulders, a burden many of them find chronically disabling. This is accomplished by the process of *scapegoating*.

Scapegoating

The historical origins of this process lie thousands of years back in the religious rituals of the Old Testament. On Yom Kippur (the Jewish Day of Atonement) the High Priest was instructed to take two male goats, one for ritual slaughter, and the other (the scapegoat) to be sent out into the wilderness, bearing the sins of the children of Israel. The ancient Greeks had a practice of using human scapegoats to ward off plagues and other calamities. A man and a woman would be driven around the town, beaten with twigs and stones before being expelled from the city.

The idea, therefore, of a 'scapegoat' which carries responsibility for the faults of others has come down to us from ancient history. It is still operating in human societies today whenever an innocent person is unjustly punished for crimes he or she did not commit, or when we must place blame upon someone for the ills of either family or society. We seem to need someone to carry the can, and sometimes it does not matter who that 'someone' is – an individual, a group of individuals or even a whole nation, 'the enemy'. Herein lies the origin of much of the suspicion between nations involved in the former East–West 'cold war'. How does this 'scapegoating' work in family situations?

The starting point is often found in the need to pass on the blame for painful experiences to other people, even those (or especially those) within one's own family. It is a common experience in marital therapy for one spouse to say, in all seriousness, that the blame for the unhappy state of affairs within their marriage is all their partner's fault. The strange thing is that their partner tells a different story!

> How cooperative spouses or leading members of the family are, how willing they are to help and share in taking responsibility for the problems and their resolution, is itself of diagnostic importance; for example, their insistence on making one person the repository of all disturbances or blame suggests that they need to see and keep it that way. An extreme example is where a member of the family is falsely admitted to a mental hospital by relatives who want rid of him or her.
>
> (Dennis Brown and Jonathan Pedder, *Introduction to Psychotherapy*, Tavistock Publications 1979, pp. 143–4)

The dynamics behind this kind of family behaviour are not hard to understand. Sometimes it can be an unconscious process – except to the person being scapegoated! The avoidance of personal or corporate responsibility can know no bounds. It begins with a sinister game of 'pass the parcel' of the bad feelings within a family, and ultimately one member of the family gets landed with those feelings permanently. The family then has an objective 'reason' for all of its ills; 'It's *all* his/her fault!' Thus, the 'black sheep' is created (Fig. 4).

> One way of looking at it is that they redraw the *family* boundary so that the scapegoat is now outside it. Everyone else in the family is now 'good', while the scapegoat contains all the badness, and 'causes all the trouble' that the family suffers. And, of course, since the scapegoat is now such a 'bad' person, it gives everyone else the chance to express all their bad feelings – with the excuse that it is all the scapegoat's fault that they are having to behave so badly towards him or her.
>
> (Robin Skynner and John Cleese, *Families and How to Survive Them*, Methuen 1983, p. 106)

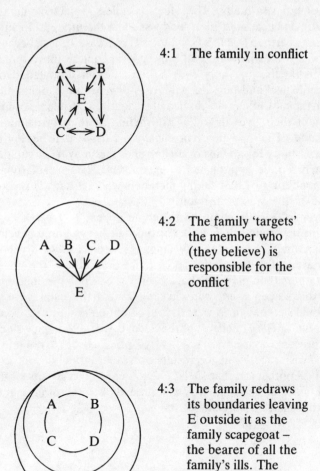

4:1 The family in conflict

4:2 The family 'targets' the member who (they believe) is responsible for the conflict

4:3 The family redraws its boundaries leaving E outside it as the family scapegoat – the bearer of all the family's ills. The conflict ceases

Fig. 4 The scapegoating process

Many people who are sent out into the 'wilderness' in this way 'die' there, not physically (though this may perhaps be true for some) but spiritually. They feel worthless, rejected and the 'reason' is because of their 'badness': like the little girl in Jules Feiffer's cartoon ('That's how I found out I wasn't good, because if I was good why would all these good people want to punish me?'), like the goat in the Jewish ritual, they are despatched to a psychological and physical wilderness where the 'badness' laid upon them by others weighs heavily. Clearly, such people cannot live out their lives in joyful affirmation of their own unique selfhood. They are now chronically *predisposed* to accepting responsibility for any ills or misfortunes that may be circulating in their families unattached to anyone else. They regularly get 'dumped' on by other family members who act out the sinister game of 'If it weren't for you!'

Even physically some such people appear to have a huge weight tied round their necks or on their backs, some develop stoops which, in terms of body language, depict (outwardly) how they are feeling (inwardly) about themselves. Truly, the sins of the fathers (and mothers) have been visited upon the children.

If this 'scapegoating' were the only result of the blaming game, it would be enough to warrant our attention and to seek some remedies. (The Holocaust of the Second World War shows how this process was used as a political weapon, in order to obliterate the Jewish race.) But the results of 'scapegoating' do not stop there. Another familiar social phenomenon emerges out of the experience of being unfairly and unjustly accused of actions of which we are entirely innocent – guilt.

3

The Question of Guilt

Guilt, strangely enough, is essentially 'user-friendly', like pain. That is not the same as saying it is *pleasant*; far from it. But guilt, like other forms of pain in the human organism, is a friendly warning to us that something is wrong and needs our attention. In the case of guilt, we receive strong signals from our inner world, where our moral guidance system resides, that *there is conflict within us*. If we could reduce this conflict to the proportions of a Walt Disney movie, and see it animated, we could imagine the Keeper of our Moral Conscience telling an errant husband, 'You've just broken the rules you gave me years ago. You've always prided yourself on your honesty – and now you've just lied to your wife about that girl at the office party! I can't cope with your mixed messages. Are you listening to me?'

Acknowledging real guilt

Such a message would be interpreted by psychologists as real or appropriate guilt. Indeed, were such a message *not* to be given there would be something drastically wrong. This form of guilt challenges this husband to:

- listen to the message
- acknowledge the conflict
- admit to the uncomfortable feelings associated with guilt
- decide whether to tell his wife or not
- if not, he would suffer from a 'guilty conscience'.

Either way, this man was bound to 'suffer', either by admitting his guilt or by concealing it. Both cause pain. The first option, however, could lead to a reconciliation with both his wife and his conscience; the second option would ensure that the guilt would continue to trouble him.

33

There are many events in our lives when we can recall such struggles with our moral guidance system, our conscience. The MP Harriet Harman once wrote: 'The Beast of guilt is always lurking around the corner ready to leap out at you if anything goes wrong' (*Observer Magazine*, 13 November 88). She struggles with her duties as a mother of three small children and her career as a member of Parliament. When all is going well at home, she says, 'I am absolutely fine.' But if anything did go wrong, for instance, if her children started to fall behind at school, 'I would blame myself because everyone would blame me.'

This kind of guilt is the result of the conflict beneath the surface (but which can emerge quickly into painful consciousness), as if the organism is saying, 'Look, you're going into overload; you're giving me two messages which I'm finding it hard to cope with: your duty to your children versus your duty as an MP.' Add to that equation other calls upon Harriet Harman's time, such as her husband and her own free time for herself, and it is not difficult to discover where feelings of guilt come from. We are trying to get the balance of life right; we are trying to put all the claims upon our time and energy into a working relationship. And it does not always work satisfactorily.

But the feelings of guilt still remain friendly. They are part of our support system, overriding our attempts to stifle them. Such feelings come from that part of our own inner wisdom, which 'knows best' and is not slow in telling us so. You cannot *will* guilty feelings away; they call for attention and we remain miserable until we respond.

Guilt is a device our inner wisdom uses to call for *action*, but guilty feelings cannot tell us what action to take. They only make us aware that something, somehow, needs attention. They identify the scenario, but cannot write the script; they make the diagnosis, but do not give the prescription.

What can we do with this kind of appropriate guilt?

The temptation, of course, is to bury it. 'Forget it; have another drink. Don't get morbid' says the optimist within. So we try for a while distraction, or busyness or denial. We put on the false grin, as if all is well, though we know damn well it is not. Chronic blamesters, of course, have been playing the game so long they are no longer aware of the possibility that they could be in the wrong. They develop a thick skin, becoming insensitive to any form of personal liability or fault. They have 'screened out' any messages from their internal moral guidance system, and only the faults of aliens appear on the screen! Is there an alternative way of dealing with real guilt?

Overcoming real guilt

Maybe a map would help to identify the process of treating real or appropriate guilt, that is, some wrong we have done or some right we have not done (Fig. 5).

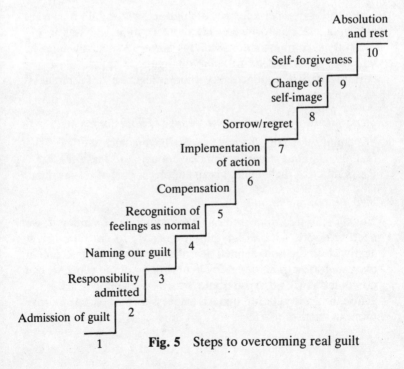

Fig. 5 Steps to overcoming real guilt

Step one: admission of guilt

We must admit our wrongdoing to ourselves. This is vital. We need to stop playing games with ourselves and making excuses ('If it weren't for him . . .' or, 'If I hadn't got out of bed that day it would never have happened!'). The plain fact of the matter is that 'it' did happen, and we helped to make 'it' happen.

Step two: admitting responsibility

We must admit that we are responsible for what happened. Depending on that undefined 'it', we may only have to admit a *part* of the responsibility, whatever we honestly feel we are responsible for.

Step three: naming our guilt

I recall an American colleague of mine at the hospital I worked in as chaplain talking to me one day about a patient who was having difficulty in coming to terms with his cancer, 'When you name it, you own it!' We need to *name* our guilt. 'I am guilty of . . . betrayal of trust, unpunctuality, thoughtlessness, unfaithfulness' – or whatever. Just own it!

Step four: recognizing that our feelings of guilt are normal

We should not punish ourselves for having such feelings. The feelings of guilt are punishment enough, at least for now. Responding to such feelings is an important part of self-healing.

Step five: compensation

Having admitted to ourself our wrongdoing, and naming it, we need to decide what, if anything we can do to put things right again. Here the now-defined 'it' will probably come into one of two categories: those things or circumstances about which we can do something; and those about which we cannot. This is the action that guilt calls for, and it is a necessary part of the recovery process.

Step six: implementing action

If our guilt comes into the category of things about which we can do something, we need to decide what that something might be. For example, is it an unreserved apology ('I'm sorry I was late; it was entirely my fault'), or, is it some act of restitution, for instance, paying back money we stole or to which we were not entitled? Where there is reparable damage of some kind, this can be a matter of negotiation between us and the injured party. Whatever we feel we need to do is the next step on our map of recovery.

Step seven: expressing sorrow and regret

If our guilt comes into the category of those things about which, practically, we can do nothing, a further need arises. Suppose, for example, we have let someone down, forgotten an appointment or anniversary, or accidentally destroyed something that is irreplaceable. We feel stuck with our guilt. I recall a couple on a television show where the wife, every time they argued, would bring up the fact that her husband failed to get to the hospital in time for their son's birth. There was no way in which that husband could ever make amends – he could not put the clock back and have a second opportunity! When such events concern other people, perhaps all we can do is to express sorrow and remorse for our actions.

Step eight: changing our self-image

It is important that we connect our wrongdoings to our ability as human beings to make mistakes: 'To err is human . . .' We can make a serious reappraisal of ourselves, and discover, if we have never done so before, that we are, after all, as fallible as anyone else. Our image of superman/superwoman needs urgent adjustment. This is not the same as making excuses for ourselves! To be able to say, 'I guess I'm as capable as anyone else of making mistakes', is to recognize that we will not always get things right, in spite of our attempts as nice, decent people to do so. I need to adjust my expectations of myself to include the possibility of error. (I needed to say just that to myself last week, when I 'crashed' an entire chapter of this book by pressing the wrong key on my word processor!) Only after admitting our errors and naming them can we make this adjustment, otherwise it would seem that we are merely shrugging our shoulders and protesting, 'Anyone can make a mistake!' That is an excuse, not a confession, of my fallible humanity.

Step nine: self-forgiveness

This step concerns the vital need for forgiveness by others and by ourselves. We need to experience *both* kinds of forgiveness in order to heal our brokenness. What is forgiveness? It is certainly not to be confused with a casual, 'Oh, don't mention it. Forget it!' Forgiveness is the voluntary act of relinquishing a rightful claim upon other people (or ourselves) and a refusal to hold that act, which prompted the need for forgiveness, against them (or ourselves) any longer. Forgiveness is the final act of healing the guilt. We can stop beating ourselves over the head for our faults, or treating ourselves as our worst enemy. We can forgive ourselves. We can stop blaming ourselves. We can rest.

Step ten: absolution and rest

Some people, and I do realize that this may not appeal to all, will need some formal or religious act of confession to help in this recovery process from guilt. The confessional nature of the Christian faith in its liturgy and worship has been of immense help to many struggling pilgrims. The general confession and its subsequent absolution can calm the mind and the heart, as an objective declaration of God's forgiveness of the penitent. Such an objective experience of absolution can aid the penitent's task of self-forgiveness.

Overcoming criminal guilt

But what happens when our guilt is criminal guilt? Criminal guilt brings us into another, more complicated, dimension. This time we are involved in the legal process of our country, where our

38

actions are questioned in the full glare of publicity. It is not now a question of our privately putting things right with the person we have wronged, although this could be one of the Court's stipulations. We may be called upon to pay appropriate damages. Neither is it merely a question of our having bad feelings about what we have done wrong. We are now to be held publicly accountable for our actions, with the full process of the law brought to bear upon us. We have not just offended against another person; we have broken the law of our land.

Paradoxically, in the majority of cases, when the culprit is brought to book, and an appropriate punishment meted out by the courts, overcoming criminal guilt is easier. One can never expunge the guilty act, never put the clock back and have another chance of writing our personal history. What is done is done. But there is a sense of having 'paid' for our offences once our punishment, be it a fine or imprisonment, is over and done with. It is at least possible to start our lives over again, without the necessity of a nagging conscience to hamper us. Having met the law's demands, we have accomplished everything that could possibly be done. We do not have to sentence ourselves to a lifetime of self-blame and self-recrimination. We may have to carry the stigma of our crime, but we do not have to carry a burden of guilt. It is possible for us to leave the guilty feelings behind us. Whether criminal or not, it is possible for guilt to be dissolved in the soothing waters of self-forgiveness.

So the 'ex-con' is able to take his or her place in the community again. Just because they made one mistake does not mean that they have to pay for it for the rest of their lives. The energy previously used in blaming themselves for what they did, and about which they can now do nothing more, is thereby released and diverted into the building of a new life and new relationships. By performing the demands of the law, we have paid our dues. While many of the points in the ten-step 'map' (Fig. 5; pp. 35–8) still apply here, I would like to add some specific factors in this special treatment of criminal guilt. The rehabilitation of offenders is seen in most cultures as a desirable good.

In outline, I offer the following response for consideration by all who are concerned with the wholeness of people in pain. I believe that a therapeutic response to those suffering from the aftermath of criminal guilt needs to include the following issues:

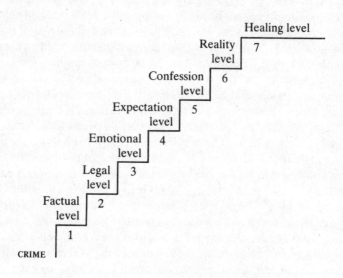

Fig. 6 Steps to overcoming criminal guilt

The factual level

This is a full and honest retelling of their story, what happened to whom, where and when and how. (As in surgery, it is often necessary to open old wounds where there are still sources of infection that prevent healing.)

The legal level

What, if anything, has been done by way of meeting the demands of society's system of justice? Have they paid the fine, 'done their time' and fulfilled all the obligations of law? (Healing does not have to await the cessation of such punishment; it can and often does begin in prison.)

The emotional level

How does the offender *feel* about what happened? What are the feelings still left long after the event itself? How has their crime left them feeling about themselves? These feelings need full expression.

The expectation level

What is the guilty person looking for? What does 'help' look like to them? How would they like life to be at the end of the healing process? What are they hoping for? (This needs checking out by reality-testing; any hopes that they can reverse what took place need to be abandoned.)

The confession level

There needs to be a full admission of their actual guilt and an expression of their sadness, remorse, sorrow and pain about what they did. Repentance needs to be verbalized. (Some might find it helpful, depending on the background of each person, to find a religious context in which this can take place such as a formal confession to a priest or minister of the church.)

The reality level

Much work may have to be done by way of change to the offender's self-image. Pleas of, 'How could I have done such a thing? It wasn't like me at all!' need to be met with a calm presentation of the facts. Any resistances they still exhibit to accepting into their self-image such evil, or weakness, as their crime evidenced, need to be confronted. 'The truth seems to be that there is part of you that *is* perfectly capable of such appalling things' may be one therapeutic response. They need to accept that as true of them.

The healing level

Finally, there is the need for self-forgiveness. This is perhaps the hardest part of all, but without this the person is condemned to a life of chronic guilt and personal impairment. Having done all that the law demands, made restitution, admitted their guilt and their feelings of sorrow, and received into their conscious awareness the hard truth that they are human and thus capable of wrong, they need to forgive *themselves*. This is not a cosy option (as anyone who has ever tried it will have found). In real terms, it means ceasing the 'self-blaming game'. It means abandoning the constant self-scourging for the past, and working towards an understanding that forgiveness is unconditional love. When we reach this we have reached the level of healing.

Whether or not these steps in the treatment of criminal guilt are thought of as naive or unworkable, I hope that they may at least provide a workable agenda to be addressed by those in the helping professions. I would welcome improvements to my list.

If we take the healing, and reinstatement, of human beings seriously we dare not dodge the hard cases. Healing does not mean perfection; it does involve facilitating people to live their lives to the maximum level of enjoyment and creativity and dignity. This cannot be achieved when we play the blaming game, either with ourselves or other people. It is precisely because the blaming game is so negative and destructive, and ultimately conducive to maximizing human pain, misery and distress, that all who are serious about improving the quality of human existence need to give it fuller attention. We will examine more of the effects of blaming in Chapter 4.

False (neurotic) guilt

But what can we do about the false, neurotic guilt mentioned earlier?

Some of the 'guilty feelings' we get, however, are not based on any real or objective wrong we have committed. Sometimes our consciences give us 'false messages', rather like getting a bug in a computer; it simply screws everything up. But where do such bugs come from?

We know from psychological studies that it is quite possible to confuse our inner moral guidance system by receiving false information. Such confusion is called 'conditioning' or 'programming'. Many people suffer from 'conditioned guilt' – they feel guilty not because they have done anything wrong; they have merely been *trained* to feel that way about certain actions or behaviour. Feeling guilty can become a habit. (Actress Maureen Lipman includes 'full time guilt' amongst her recreations in *Who's Who*.)

Take sex as a good example of this process. One of the firmly held beliefs when I was a lad was that masturbation would make you go blind! Clearly, this personal sexual activity was being put forward as a dangerous 'no-go' area, and many myths abound concerning the dangers of indulging its strong impulse. More people feel guilty about sex than any other human activity. You may recall some of the injunctions (now thought totally ludicrous) concerning sexual activity which, at the time they were conveyed to you, were regarded as divine law! While there may have been a beneficent motive on the part of our parents, nevertheless the outcome of much so-called 'sex education' is to make us feel as guilty as hell. Such 'conditioned guilt', 'false guilt' or 'phoney guilt', rather than a breach of some moral law of the universe, boils down to 'What would Mum/Dad think if they knew. . .?' In this case, 'wrongdoing' must be translated into 'things Mum and Dad would not approve of'. As mature adults, we need to recognize that many of our concepts of right and wrong originate in the preferences of our parents for an easy (or at least respectable) life! Some actions designated as 'sin' are quite possibly only what proved to be inconvenient to our parents.

We are now able to appreciate how these psychological bugs got into our system, and what the process of conditioning is and how it works. We are now on the track of these 'false messages' which were programmed into our system, but we need to know 'Why?' Sam Keen tells us:

A child needs to dwell in a garden of innocence. . . . From the

43

beginning, it is tutored in the orthodox and righteous distinction between good and evil. The home is the first church and school. The tension and relaxation of muscles, smiles and frowns, teach us Father's and Mother's philosophy of right and wrong. . . . The anxiety caused by the threat of abandonment or punishment keeps us within the walls of the garden. An invisible electric fence of conscience, an unconscious barrier enforced by shame and guilt, keeps us within predetermined boundaries. In childhood we remain within the circle of familiar love because, fearful of the terrors that may lurk in the unknown darkness, we are drawn by the warmth and light of the hearth. Right or wrong, good or evil, obedience or disobedience, love or abandonment, acceptance or guilt, approval or shame – these form the boundaries within which the psyche of the child finds security, trust and courage.

(The Passionate Life, Gateway Books 1985, p. 42)

So it appears that our very necessary survival instincts can serve to maintain the programme of false guilt. In our childlike state of dependence upon parental nurture, conformity was all that stood between us and abandonment. Given the choice between conditional acceptance in the garden, and unconditional rejection outside, we will usually choose the former. That way we stay alive; we survive. But we pay a price for this survival. Our original acceptance of our own self-worth and innocence has to make way for the price of acceptance: denial of our self. Our convictions about the goodness and rightness of sexual expression must give way to a perverted and distorted alien transplant of shame and guilt.

It is but a short step from this denial of our essential goodness to an affirmation of our own essential badness. Having denied our own true selves in the vital interests of survival, we find ourselves burdened with self-doubt. The true *me* has had to be suppressed, and I am conditioned to believe it to be *not-me*. The present me that now appears is my conditioned, parent-manufactured, '*not-self*' – a contrivance produced by my need to survive and to avoid abandonment. A switch has taken place so that when I dare to listen to the calling of my true (suppressed) me, I must learn to deny that part of myself as sinful, suspect and even 'of the Devil'! It is at this point that some of the history of the Christian Church has much to answer for.

Although the modern sexual revolution broke the mould of medieval repression, it brought other problems in its wake. While it had the effect of divorcing guilt from sex, it also separated sex from love and commitment. In recent years, of course, AIDS has also focused the mind on the responsibility now attached to easy sex. However, there seems to be no call for a return to the outdated puritanism of the past, except by some fringe elements of the church.

There are, of course, other areas of human experience that can be used in the processes of 'conditioned guilt' – food, for example (cream cakes, hisses the ad-man, are 'naughty but nice!'). The cult of slimness is as likely to bring about a guilty conscience as the pleasure of a total orgasm, especially among women (to whom most of the advertising is addressed). The latest inducement to breast-beating comes from the advent of Green products. Woe betide us if we are still using CFC-type sprays. Small is apparently now not beautiful, unless it runs on unleaded petrol. The use of guilt is by no means a thing of the past as a stimulus to change and conformity – however valid the pragmatic arguments might be.

Survivor's guilt: a modern example of false guilt

This facet of guilt receives wide publicity following the investigation of every national and international tragedy. As the personal stories begin to emerge in the aftermath of some tragic event, a specific form of guilt can be identified. It is called 'survivor's guilt', and it is by no means new.

It was recognized, for instance, as a significant element in the treatment of the survivors of the Nazi concentration camps following the Second World War. Survivor's guilt emerged as those feelings of unworthiness, shame and guilt for having survived the conflict while millions of people did not. The presence of survivor's guilt is betrayed by the questions that the survivors of a tragedy sometimes ask. 'Why didn't I die as well as my wife?' 'Why should I survive when my children died?' 'I don't deserve to live; my husband was a better person than I am!' 'Why did I escape?'

Similar things are said by the survivors of any contemporary disaster, whether they be air, land or sea accidents. Such issues are always part of the agenda during the recovery process, especially where this takes place in a therapeutic context.

The same is true for the rescuers involved in the recovery work. They, too, often experience feelings of worthlessness. 'I should have saved more people' they will tell you. They will dismiss the value of what they did do, and only emphasize what they did *not* do. This is a form of 'survivor's guilt'.

At the rational level, none of these brave men and women has anything to reproach themselves for; but then the problem is not at a rational level. The underlying problem surrounding 'survivor's guilt' is an emotional, not a rational one. In various ways, these people are part of the blaming game, blaming themselves unnecessarily for the fact that they survived when others did not. Ultimately, they need to be brought to see that their feelings are entirely natural, and that they have internalized something that needs to be externalized. This can sometimes be accomplished by a reliving – under clinical conditions – of the original trauma, in order to release the repressed emotions that could not be expressed at the time. This is a long-term therapeutic task; the survivor's guilt is merely an unconscious method of keeping such feelings of horror and terror buried within themselves.

Overcoming false guilt

An example may help.

Case history : Louise

Louise and her sister lived at home with their mother and

father. Her parents' marriage was in ruins: constant rows leading nowhere, threats and occasions of violence, general unhappiness all round. Mother moved out into the spare room. Eventually the older sister left home. When Louise was 15, she was awoken one night by an argument outside her bedroom door. Her father had come home drunk, and was demanding sex from his wife. She refused. Apparently the father had then threatened to rape Louise if the wife still refused him sex. Meanwhile, Louise lay in her bed absolutely terrified. Somehow, her mother managed to talk her husband out of his intention, but was heard to tell him that as soon as Louise left home for university, she would leave as well.

Louise never forgot that evening. Not wishing her parents to separate, she began to put off all thoughts of going to university, although this is what she wanted more than anything else. What should she do?

Eventually, she decided that she would risk applying for a university place, and was awarded a scholarship to Cambridge. During her first term, her mother left home.

Louise blamed herself. It was all her fault that her parents' marriage had broken up. 'After all,' she said, 'if I hadn't gone to university, my parents would still be together.' She was plagued with feelings of guilt.

When she came to see me, she was on the verge of giving up her studies in the hope that, by returning home, her mother would follow suit. She did not want to leave Cambridge but it seemed to her the only way to deal with her guilt complex.

Now it may be clear to you that Louise was *not* responsible for the breakup of her parents' marriage, but she could not be convinced of that. This 'false guilt' was in fact masking her own grief. She eventually got in touch with those feelings, and began to see that the separation was in fact her parents' choice. By going back home, she would merely be manipulating her mother to return to a situation which, for her, was intolerable. On top of that, her mother would then be feeling guilty for having caused her daughter to give up her studies, and so the disease of false guilt would be spread even further.

Gradually, Louise made some decisions for herself:

- not to take responsibility for the choice of her parents
- not to accept the blame for Mother leaving the family home
- not to be used as a pawn in the family games
- to express her natural anger at her parents for having placed on her shoulders the future of their marriage
- she had nothing to feel guilty about
- she was entitled to choose what she wanted to do
- she could own her true feelings of sadness concerning her parents
- she could finally give up feeling guilty.

The lengths to which some people will go to maintain their imagined guilt is quite considerable. Guilt complexes are often resistant to entreaty or explanation. The trick is to get to the feelings *beneath* the feelings of guilt (in Louise's case, these were sadness and anger) and find appropriate ways of expressing them. Feelings connected to imagined (or conditioned) guilt are usually a substitute for other, unfocused feelings (this also applies to survivor's guilt).

Since such imagined guilt is not real, forgiveness is not the cure. Forgiveness only works where there are real or appropriate feelings of guilt. Dr Paul Tournier writes,

> The answer to their anxiety is psychological, not religious; it ought to be exoneration rather than forgiveness. The anxiety is due, in fact, not to a fault or a sin for which they ought to be blamed, but to an injury of which they have been the victims. Forgiveness is needed only where guilt can be attributed.
>
> (*The Strong and the Weak*, SCM 1974, p. 221)

These are important words. People who cling on to false beliefs about themselves, whether of excessive goodness or excessive badness, are always living lives that are essentially broken to some degree. There seem to be limitless ways of proving to other people that we are 'bad', 'worthless', 'guilty', or just plain 'no good'. There are, of course, elements of self-protection in some forms of self-blaming. If we have such a bad image of ourselves, other people may think twice before adding to it! Or, we might use such a ploy as a form of retaliation against others: 'Look what you've done to me!' Continual self-recrimination in a marriage can destroy it, and it is hard not to see, on occasions, a subconscious desire to do so. Having driven the partner to distraction and to an abandonment of the marriage, the neurotically guilty person can simply add to the list of 'proofs' that they are worthless: 'You see, even he recognized my worthlessness in the end!'

Such people are not guilty; they are sick. As Dr Tournier says, such people do not need forgiveness; they need some form of therapy, especially as such symptoms often form part of a depressive illness. 'But where do I begin?' you may ask. Your local doctor would be a good place to start, especially if you have a good relationship with him or her. If not, talk this over with a trusted friend who will listen to what you have to say. But if you have no such person, agencies such as the Samaritans or local counselling centres are always willing to listen to you. (There are some addresses at the end of this book which could form useful starting places for some of you who feel isolated and alone.)

4

The Effects of Unfair Blaming

We have already noticed the distinction between real and false blame. While blaming other people, and ourselves, can be the honest and real thing to do, there is another feature of human behaviour that perverts this appropriate use of blame into what I have called the blaming game. This sinister form of behaviour has not only a long history but devastating *effects*.

False innocence

One of these effects is to reinforce the gamester's sense of false innocence. If they can persuade others that they are in the wrong, then they stay in the right, which merely serves to spread even further the results of their own myopic, or possibly perverted attitude to life. Those who go in for the art of 'blamesmanship' are responsible for much of this world's moral and psychological pollution. They become hardened to any truth about themselves. Such is the twisted belief in their own self-righteousness that they are deaf and blind to the truth; ultimately, they become bigots and tyrants. They are the faultfinders of our world, ready to attribute responsibility right, left or centre – anywhere but to themselves. They are hyper-critical of other people and their efforts. They live shrouded in a blanket of negativity; they are the detractors in our family or social groupings. Nothing positive ever issues forth from their mouths; they are only opened in condemnation of other people's actions, against which (of course) their own shine brightly! In the end they become thoroughly toxic.

They can pull people to pieces with a disarming smile. They put others down with consummate ease and skill; they can spot a defect at 100 metres! Their eyes are like radar beams, scanning the surrounding social atmosphere for any signs of human failure. They are past-masters (and past-mistresses) at setting up scapegoats. They have an uncanny instinct for knowing who is to blame, with a certainty that is as breathtaking as it is arrogant. Since such people are often out of touch with reality, and not conducive to change, they are best left alone. We will only become frustrated, or – worse – contaminated by their influence if we remain under it. As parents, the effect of their toxicity upon their children is well established. To be subjected to the tyranny of such self-righteous parenting is one of the most harrowing experiences that children can receive.

Many of us can see the results daily. People grow up with a distorted view of life, and especially of their own intrinsic goodness. The early optimism with which most people are born is often crushed, and they assume a gloomy, pessimistic view of life. Of course, they fight unfair blaming – at first – and protest their innocence.

Case history: Madeleine

Madeleine came to see me in deep depression, the roots of which went back to early childhood. She had been labelled the 'black sheep' of the family for as long as she could remember. Subconsciously, she had taken on the role of family hellraiser which only made her more depressed.

When she was very young – about eight or nine – she had been sexually abused by a visitor to their home. When she reported this to her parents, she was met with a blank stare, and an instant dismissal of 'such rubbish'. When Madeleine persisted, her mother would hear no more of it. 'Well, you must have encouraged him, that's all I can say!' said her mother. The burning resentment of such unfair blaming stayed with her for most of her life. It was a major factor in her subsequent depression and her difficulties in sexual relationships.

Before looking further at the consequences of this unfair blaming, it would be useful to examine where Madeleine's mother was coming from in this particular episode. What caused this massive denial of her daughter's story?

Unfair blaming doesn't just happen: it's caused. It comes out of an unwillingness to deal appropriately with life's problems. Before we condemn Madeleine's mother, let's try and put ourselves in her position for a moment. Her daughter tells of a sexual assault by a guest in their house. If her mother had taken the story seriously, it would have meant first sharing the story with her husband, and then perhaps jointly challenging their guest about his behaviour.

The immediate result would have been acute embarrassment, and this would have been entirely understandable. After all, it is not an easy thing to do, especially when you did not witness the events yourself. Supposing your daughter is telling stories: what then? What would your guest think of you, entertaining such malicious beliefs concerning his behaviour in your house? Would he not leave immediately, and a friendship end in disaster? But, on the other hand, what would your guest do if the story turned out to be true? Could Madeleine's mother deal with either her anger or her embarrassment? Could she cope with his admission of guilt, and his feelings of shame and disgust? This situation resembles the traditional 'no-win' encounter: the mother loses either way. Either she experiences shame and awkwardness in confronting the guest, or she experiences shame and awkwardness in betraying her daughter. If she stands up to the guest, she may lose a friendship whether or not he admits to the misdemeanour. The easier option is to refuse to believe the girl's story: that way, it can all be swept under the carpet and 'least said soonest mended' considered the best policy. What Madeleine's mother did not reckon on was the devastating effect this 'easy option' was to have upon her daughter's life.

Effectively it turned the girl in upon herself. No more would she look to her mother as rescuer or nurturer. Clearly (to Madeleine at any rate) her mother thought her either a liar or a temptress. She would do well to question her mother's care or interest in her welfare in the future. Madeleine would have to learn to live in a world without trusting others to support her. Worse still, her unexpressed anger at her mother and the guest would be suppressed like an internal pollutant, poisoning the inner springs of her well-being. Her later depression, suicide attempts and withdrawal from physical contact (especially sexual contact) were all the result of the unfair blaming by her mother. And what caused that unfair blaming was the least line of resistance taken by her mother. She, in this instance at any rate, failed to act appropriately towards Madeleine and ever since has wondered at her daughter's total indifference towards her. And all because of a wish to avoid shame and embarrassment! Madeleine was sacrificed upon the altar of her mother's desire not to upset a guest in her home.

William Shakespeare spoke for all victims of innocent suffering when he wrote,

A wretched soul, bruised with adversity,
We bid be quiet when we hear it cry;
But were we burdened with like weight of pain,
As much, or more, we should ourselves complain.
(*Comedy of Errors, Act II, Scene 1*)

Thousands of Madeleines have had similar experiences. Since the sexual abuse of young children gained publicity in the mid-eighties, adults (and especially those in the caring and legal professions) are ready to receive such stories with a greater degree of credibility than hitherto. Sexually abused children often display a form of guilt through inverted blame, especially when the perpetrator is their father who subsequently goes to jail. Characteristically, they carry the blame for having done something wrong, even when the truth is just the reverse. 'It's all my fault the family broke up; if I hadn't said anything, we'd still all be together.' This kind of confession is sometimes formulated by the victim of child sexual abuse precisely because of what their siblings are telling them. Such blaming is unfair and untrue.

Rape and blame

Victims of rape have also been subject to this phenomenon of unfair blaming. In spite of the enlightenment brought by the feminist movement, the traditional male understanding still remains that the rape victim 'must have asked for it'! I have counselled dozens of rape victims and, flying in the face of any evidence to support it, many of them instantly blamed themselves for what had taken place. I have heard women say:

- I should have been more careful
- It was my fault; I left the window open
- I just didn't check the locks on my front door
- If only I'd looked behind me sooner
- I must have been stupid taking that route home
- Maybe it was the dress I was wearing. . . .
- He wasn't as brutal as I had expected. . . .
- I shouldn't have been so trusting

All these statements reflect the view of the victim that they must *assume and accept some responsibility for the rape having taken place*. These victims are accepting that they were either totally or partly to blame for the rape. They feel 'responsible'.

Such a view is absolutely mistaken.

The responses quoted above come from a place within these victims which needs to make sense of what happened. This is perfectly natural considering the fundamental search for causation. In the absence of any logic, they will resort to blaming themselves. A more appropriate response is to place the blame where it actually belongs: on to the aggressor, the rapist. It is not a question of making sure doors are locked, windows closed, or the event not being as shocking as might have been expected. All these elements are irrelevant; none of them invite or justify rape.

It is completely understandable that women should ransack their brains for reasons to accuse themselves. After all, some people will still apportion some blame to them, so there is no harm in having their story ready. Because of this, many rape victims fail to report the incident, especially if they anticipate further humiliation during the judicial proceedings. 'They have to be prepared,' writes Elaine Storkey, 'for the defence lawyer to rake up any irrelevant mud in order to produce the desired image

54

of the "rape" victim as a probably promiscuous woman, and the "rape" by implication, as intercourse with consent.' (*What's Right With Feminism*, SPCK 1985, p. 39). However, the blame rests solely on the rapist; it is he, and *he alone*, who is responsible, not his mauled victims.

In the light of some recent questionable judicial decisions concerning rape cases, it is clear that there are still some people around living in the old, male-dominated world who believe that all rape victims must have asked for it. One learned (?) judge actually said that he had been lenient in his sentencing of one rapist because the victim had withstood the attack with great bravery, and it 'clearly' had not had a devastating effect on her! Whether or not the victim acts bravely, and whether or not the event had a devastating effect on her (and who is to tell the long-term results of such a trauma?) is completely beside the point. Another judge even went so far as to accuse one victim of 'contributory negligence', to the rightful outcry of many women. The *entire* blame lies with the attacker.

The results of this line of thinking are seen in victims who are left to carry some of the blame for what happened. They have *a distortion in their self-image;* some see themselves as unclean or believe that there is something wrong with them for men to want to attack them! One woman told me in a dreamy, half unreal way the story of the 'gang-bang' rape perpetrated upon her. She concluded that she must be a very bad person for that kind of thing to happen to her. God had been punishing her for something; thus, she must have deserved it!

Such conclusions, not at all uncommon in the immediate aftermath of rape, are just about as far from the truth as it is possible to travel. Much therapeutic work has to be done with such people in order to restore the truth of the situation, and to help them make a more appropriate attribution of blame from themselves to their attackers. It is not she who is bad or evil; there is nothing she has either done or failed to do which could possibly merit such an act of violence and humiliation. The total responsibility, the real guilt, lies with the rapist.

Unfair blaming

Enormous damage is done to people who wrongly ingest (through introjection) the blame for what other people do to them. Unfair blaming, therefore, is something we can do to ourselves. Such wounds are self-inflicted.

However, there are many more instances when these wounds come from those who want to 'pass the buck' of responsibility, as in rape victims. For example, husbands traditionally find it hard to understand how their wives came to be raped, particularly where there are no external signs of a struggle. While outwardly offering support, they often harbour silent questions concerning the level of their wives' cooperation. Sadly, the divorce statistics of marriages where rape has been proven are far higher than the national averages. Again, the long-term psychological damage of such blaming can be catastrophic.

A phrase which I hear many people use to describe some of their life events is, 'not fair!' By using such a phrase they are assuming that life *ought to be fair*. Often, it is not. We have been unfairly accused, wrongly punished, mistaken for someone else; our explanations or protestations of innocence have gone unheard by others. We have been condemned out of hand.

It is perfectly appropriate to declare how we *feel* about life's unfairnesses. We are only hurting ourselves unnecessarily when we take on other people's lies about who we are and what we are supposed to have done. In therapy, the client and therapist often reach a point when the truth emerges concerning a particular scenario. When examined from every angle, instead of merely the inbred view placed there by other people, or neurotic parents, a different picture begins to emerge. 'So it was not your fault, after all, when. . . .' The truth emerges very tentatively at first. A soft, apologetic whisper will agree: 'I suppose it wasn't my fault.' I then ask the client to say that again, only louder this time. I invite them to put some conviction into what they are saying. They then repeat it with more vigour: 'I suppose it wasn't my fault after all.' Now I invite them to drop the 'I suppose' bit, make it a definite statement: 'It was not my fault!' Very often, this comes out with a roar of anger and the repressed resentment that has lain dormant for years emerges in a rush of energy that takes the client by surprise: 'I didn't know how angry I felt about that, all these years.' Other clients say, over and over again, 'It's not fair!' with increasing volume. Sometimes it helps to bang a cushion while saying these words, 'It's not fair . . . it's not fair . . . it just isn't fair . . . *it's not bloody fair!* . . . How dare they. . . .' Thus the *in*rage is expressed as *out*rage.

Only those who have taken part in such therapy, either by witnessing it in others or by doing their own work, can fully appreciate the force and effectiveness of getting the record straight. People who have been carrying the can for most of their lives suddenly give the can back to the person who ought to be carrying it, and it is like lancing a boil. The ugly pus comes pouring out, and the healing process can begin. They feel free.

However, before this takes place, much of that person's life has been ruined. They have had to bear burdens that were not theirs, and they have suffered a diminishment in their natural expectation of a good life. There is no court of law to announce a judicial pardon for such people, no public announcement of their innocence, no real culprit to expose and condemn. Unfair blaming has even led to suicides, when the pain and the sheer hopelessness proved too much to bear. There was no one there to believe in them, to share their sense of outrage and humiliation. Like Madeleine, they have to bear their pain alone, and their silent resentment is turned into the raw material out of which depression emerges later in life.

We are beginning to see now the importance that unfair blaming plays in the lives of ordinary people. It lies at the root of so much human unhappiness, especially when this takes place in the most formative years of our lives. Children who grow up doubting their own essential goodness, who are systematically diminished by inadequate parenting, scapegoated by their siblings with parental connivance, cannot hope to grow up adequately as full human beings. Unless they overcome these experiences, they will suffer from emotional, if not psychological inadequacy. Many grow up to be inadequate parents themselves.

Psychological damage

What does this psychological damage consist of?

Loss of trust

There are three basic areas in which we can identify such loss of trust: towards ourselves, towards other people, and towards our world view.

I have illustrated above how unfair blaming can radically alter our opinion of ourselves. We can cease to expect any good to come from our contribution to life, since we are (so others have taught us to believe) so bad, if not evil. Some of the statements they might make include:

- I'm no good
- I'm hopeless
- I'm evil
- I am just a waste of space
- I don't know why you bother with me.

They have ceased to believe in their own value as human beings. They have no self-esteem; they are 'failures', 'rubbish', 'worthless'. They do not trust their own abilities, either to make decisions or to take any responsibility. They can become totally reliant and dependent upon others. They cease to mature.

Or they may cease to trust other people, who may be conceived as persecutors or potential accusers. People like this become very defensive, expecting to be put down – or put upon – by others. Their own hostile feelings towards themselves are projected on to others, even those around them who actually do love and respect them! 'I know you don't like me'; 'I know you don't think I'm much good as a wife!' Since their lack of trust in themselves is distorted, they live in a world full of people who are laughing at them, criticizing them, blaming them. Hence, they become suspicious, often bitter and resentful, and at times this is perfectly understandable.

This, of course, affects their view of the world as a whole. Their whole environment appears to be against them. Every event is twisted round to 'prove' that the world, fate or God, is against them. They feel accursed, predestined to pain and misery. They cannot trust their world to do them any good; vast cosmic forces seem stacked against them. Their world view is essentially negative, often reflecting how it was for them trying to survive in a toxic family.

Loss of self-esteem

A second area of psychological damage which unfair blaming raises is the loss of self-esteem.

Unfair and unjust accusation can affect the human psyche like acid rain stripping us of all beauty and assurance. It defoliates the splendour of the human spirit and destroys our true human dignity. Through unfair blaming we wither and die.

It is not only victims of rape who suffer like this. All victims of injustice and false accusation suffer to some extent. I have spoken to many of my colleagues in the world of counselling and psychotherapy who, on a regular basis, spend months, sometimes years, repairing the damage done to their clients through this particularly vicious form of attack. Through the loss of self-esteem, the belief in one's own sense of value and worth, the human spirit turns against itself. We begin to feel bad, not good about ourselves. We need to learn how to love ourselves, be kind to ourselves, accept ourselves. A major part of all counselling and psychotherapy is engaged in this important task: the restoration of the beauty and worthwhileness of human beings. They need to be helped to feel good again.

Viktor Frankl (a Viennese psychiatrist who experienced the horrors of Auschwitz and Dachau concentration camps in the Second World War) tells of his work with a Carmelite nun (in Dwight D. Cumber, 'Depression as an Ecclesiogenic Neurosis', *Journal of Pastoral Care*, December 1980, p. 256). She was seriously depressed, made more acute by the fact that depression did not fit in with her ideas of her vocation. She felt guilty and depressed about being depressed. Something was clearly (to her) lacking in her faith; otherwise, why was she depressed?

Through much patient work, Frankl managed to persuade her

to take the depression as a challenge, and she began to improve. However, one day she was visited by a priest. He told her, 'You should quit the monastery. You are not a good Carmelite because a good Carmelite can never be depressed.' Immediately, her depressive symptoms returned.

This nun was the victim of unfair accusation. The priest had delayed her inner healing by a direct statement that she was a bad Carmelite. She was being blamed for being depressed since, in the priest's eyes at least, she had no business being depressed. The gradual improvement in accepting her condition as normal and something to be worked at had now been set back almost to square one. She had lost the little self-esteem that had been gained through Frankl's intervention.

This sense of 'badness' permeates right through many people. Parents have often failed to make the important distinction between 'bad deeds' and 'bad children'. The distinction is important precisely because we often treat these two ideas as identical; in truth, they are poles apart.

We must learn to distinguish, therefore, 'doing bad' from 'being bad'. Doing bad relates to *behaviour*; being bad relates to *character*. This is why good people can do bad things at times, and it is perfectly possible to hate what people do without hating the person himself of herself. This is why we can like someone, while at the same time dislike what they are doing.

Hence, blaming phrases like, 'You're a bad boy/girl!' are received by children as absolute statements concerning, not just their behaviour, but their very constitution. What might have been intended as 'you have done a bad thing' comes across through such wanton carelessness in the use of language as 'you are a bad person'. 'Badness' becomes a concept by which those children come to identify themselves. Self-esteem is then replaced by self-loathing, self-hatred, self-denial.

Such damage is impossible to measure. Ordinary, decent parents have left their children scarred with this inheritance of psychological abuse. If they had done that kind of damage to their children's bodies, the parents would have ended up in prison. Just because such damage is inward and invisible in no way diminishes its significance. Such children will grow up with a twisted idea of their identity. Blaming children, therefore, in such a way that induces guilt and loss of self-esteem, has a great deal to answer for, and alone accounts for a large part of human misery and unhappiness.

The pursuit of misery

Another effect of unjust blaming is seen in the way some children grow up as hellraisers. 'If they think I'm bad, I'll act bad. I may as well be hung for a sheep as a lamb!'

Our borstals and other corrective institutions abound with young people who appear to be entirely without control or scruples. Sociologists refer to them as 'antisocial'; psychologists call them 'sociopaths'. They produce mayhem wherever they go, and they are by no means confined to the football terraces. Hooliganism as a social phenomenon is very complex, but some of the roots are found in the way these young people were treated in their childhood. On examination, many of them are found to have been psychologically abused as young children; moved from pillar to post, in and out of care, rootless, angry and miserable. They are regarded as the dross of human society, 'the dregs of our world', 'the scum of the earth', as intrinsically bad, a nuisance, no good; a self-fulfilling prophecy. Bad they are, so bad they become.

Whenever you can get close enough to such people, another part of their story may emerge: of pain and abandonment, of lovelessness and rejection, of desperate yearning and longing (literally, *be-longing*), for attachment and acceptance. The precipitating factors of their condition are related in all their raw and painful reality. This is not to excuse hooliganism, but it puts antisocial behaviour in a context of a *failure to love*.

There are bound to be exceptions to any causal explanations. Sometimes, hellraisers come from homes where, to all appearances, there was no failure to love. Other factors, perhaps, intervened, such as undue influence of others, or a need to break out of the mores of their upbringing. The point I am making is that once a person is branded, labelled, stigmatized, it is that much harder to reach them. Often, they will simply live out the poor expectations others have placed upon them. Sociopaths are notoriously resistant to any therapeutic process.

Blaming has a large part to play in such behaviour patterns. These people seem to go out into the world in order to pursue unhappiness, their own and that of those around them. Unhappy themselves, robbed of purpose, love and a sense of their own self-esteem and worth, they *choose* to make life miserable. 'If I'm going to suffer, others can suffer too!' The idea of paying back the world for the apparent mistreatment of themselves is not so farfetched as it may sound. The proverbial 'chip-on-the-shoulder' is a familiar enough experience to alert us to what is going on.

What, therefore, began as a private and personal deprivation of a sense of worth, goodness and value as a child, spawns an enormous social problem in our time. Marauding hordes of young people regularly create mayhem in our inner cities, and even in hitherto quiet backwaters of the countryside. It is easy to lose sight of the individual pain and need in such young people when it is our house they are smashing up, our car being vandalized, or our daughter being raped.

Stricter laws, and more severe punishment, might well be needed as deterrents to such appalling behaviour. Our sense of justice would demand this. However, natural justice also demands that the birthright of every child to love, warmth, acceptance and nurture is also placed higher on the social and national agenda.

We cannot simply address the question of the pursuit of happiness until we pay attention to the human forces which are at work producing the very misery that happiness is supposed to replace. Our habitual way of avoiding such a painful analysis is simply to blame other people; to be sure, many of them bear serious responsibility for the physical and emotional harm they do. But there is another area of responsibility, that of the parents of such children; again and again in therapy when the roots of such antisocial behaviour are uncovered, it is a painful story of systematic destruction of what was once a young and optimistic life.

A friend of mine, Chris Sparks, relates an experience he had as a young curate. On a visit to a hospital he noticed a child, listless and grey, in a sterile glass cubicle. The child's notes said, 'Failure to thrive'. He had guessed the boy to be eighteen months old; he was, in fact, three years old. The medics were baffled. The parents, he was told, can come as often as they like, but they come only once a month and stay for five minutes. My friend asked what the child's prospects were. 'His parents have no interest in him. Their monthly visits are just a matter of form. Why they come at all I can't imagine. The prognosis is very poor, in fact we think he will die.'

The death of the spirit is not just rhetoric. Of course, not every parent treats his or her child as these parents did. But the story illustrates, in a stark and unmistakable way, the kind of death of the human spirit that leaves a grown-up person (should they indeed survive at all) with a severely crippled personality pattern.

Summary

The effects of unfair blaming are, of course, far wider than I have suggested above. Each of us could share, given the right circumstances, our own painful experiences. To be scapegoated, treated as worthless and 'bad', and thought to be the 'cause' of all our family's ills, is an intolerable burden for any of us to bear. Worse still, such damage can be converted into rage and bitterness against the world *as a whole*. Thus blame turns full circle, and gets fed back into society. Sam Keen comments: 'The degree to which people blame is the degree to which they are still developmentally stuck in their family of origin; i.e. are still children. To blame is to deny both one's responsibility and one's potency.' (*Faces of the Enemy,* Harper & Row 1986, p. 21)

To live a blame-free (not to be confused with a blame*less*) life means growing up. In order to become 'blame-free', we need to become 'game-free,' and that involves a clear understanding of how games are played out. So in Chapter 5 we turn to an exploration of the gaming process.

5

The Gaming Process

Defining the gaming process

Time was when a game could be described as an activity to be enjoyed for the fun and amusement it afforded to its participants. 'Fun and games' were jovial activities in which the main aim was the sheer pleasure it gave to those taking part, and the 'game-watching' spectators.

The continuing popularity of games is evidenced in the many television programmes using the gaming format. Quiz shows, especially those involving families, have millions of viewers. And that is not surprising when you realize that the word 'game' has its origin in the idea of *fellowship*, doing things together and structuring our time in order to find enjoyment in the company of others.

However, somewhere along the linguistic process the emphasis began to shift on to another, less humorous use of the word 'game'. For example, life itself was encompassed in the idea of 'playing the game, chaps!' This was the equivalent of 'keeping to the rules' of chivalry and sportsmanship. It was almost synonymous with the British way of life, and its ideals of fairness spread around the world.

A further, non-sporting use of the word 'game' arrived with its association with 'scheme' or 'intrigue'. 'That's stopped his little game!' meant not a counterattack in chess, for example, but the thwarting and frustration of someone else's scheme against us. Playing this kind of game, therefore, became associated with the psychological defeat of our partner or enemy. A game now had more to do with dodges, tricks and stratagems ('None of your little games!') than fun. What began as friendly, or at least fair competitiveness ended in all-out war. Gone was the spirit of the Olympic Games, where the honour of taking part, not winning, is the main impetus. We soon discovered 'gamesmanship' (Stephen Potter's word) which had nothing to do with 'sport'.

Berne's Games People Play

This new aspect of 'game-playing' was the special study of the American psychiatrist, Eric Berne. He studied medicine at McGill University, Montreal, and psychiatry at Yale. In 1964 he published his most popular book, *Games People Play*, when for the first time, at a popular level, the sinister side of human game-playing was given a psychological framework. This book became a bestseller in the 1960s, and Berne's treatment of analysing human relationships (which he called *transactional analysis)* became part of the rising pop-psychology of the 1960s.

For the first time, in any depth, Berne took the lid off the ugly side of scheming that goes on between people, or groups of people, in order to reveal what was *really* taking place in human interactions. Berne produced a catalogue of games people play, albeit unconsciously. He drew attention to 'Life Games' ('Alcoholic'), 'Marital Games' ('The Frigid Woman'), 'Party Games' ('Ain't it Awful?') and even 'Consulting Room Games' ('I'm only trying to help you').

Part of the appeal of Berne's work was the way in which he reduced the concepts of his approach to just about five words: 'script', 'game', 'parent', 'adult', 'child'. While an oversimplification, this brief description includes the foundation on which a more sophisticated system of understanding human interactions could be based. Even the most uninformed reader could identify with Berne's descriptions of what people get up to with one another. He provided us with a map by which we could chart our progress through the otherwise inexplicable tangle of human relationships.

So, as we continue in our understanding of the blaming game it is important that we have this special use of the word *game* in mind:

A game is the process of doing something with an ulterior motive that:

- is outside of adult awareness
- does not become explicit until the participants switch the way they are behaving
- results in everyone feeling confused, misunderstood, and wanting to blame the other person.

  (I. Stewart and V. Joines, *TA Today*, Lifespace Publishing 1987, p. 242-3)

The payoff principle

Since these kinds of psychological games are not for fun, why are they played? More personally, why do *we* play them?

Essential to the practice of game-playing is the continuation of ruses that used to work for us when we were children. Games are essentially a throwback to the way we learned to operate when we were young. For example, a woman I spoke with complained of a habit in her marriage that was causing both her and her husband problems. Whenever they rowed, she would go silent. And the process would unfold like this:

1. Husband starts a row (sometimes quite a legitimate complaint against her).
2. She feels embarrassed, and goes silent.
3. Husband cannot stand silence.
4. Husband feels guilty that he has hurt his wife.
5. Wife blames husband (silently) for upsetting her.
6. Since this is 'all the husband's fault', it is also his responsibility for making her feel better again.
7. Wife sits it out – often for days – in silence.
8. Husband, driven up the wall by the silence, capitulates.
9. Husband admits to being in the wrong, asks for forgiveness.
10. Wife 'graciously' forgives him!

Where did the wife learn this habit, I wondered. 'This is exactly what I saw my Mum doing with my Dad,' she said; 'it always seemed to work then, but I don't feel very good about it now!'

The wife's 'silence', then, was not her problem; it was her solution. The important phrase is, 'It always seemed to work then', back in her childhood, and she is repeating a pattern learned in childhood. But she got it from her parents, so where did they get it from? Probably from *their* parents!

The payoff for this woman (and her mother) would include:

1. Not having to confront her husband's justifiable complaints.
2. Not having to justify her behaviour, however unreasonable.
3. Placing responsibility for her feelings on to her husband.
4. Making the husband responsible for putting things right.
5. Forcing the husband to back down, even to admit to being in the wrong.
6. Keeping all the power in her hands.
7. Staying in control.

The wife receives this formidable array of benefits from her pattern of behaviour, and she is not going to relinquish these lightly. Such a list of 'payoffs' always represents the *investment* in the game she is playing, which we might call 'screw you!' She knows the husband's weak spot (he cannot abide silence) and she works on this in order to bring him back to heel once more.

Silence is an integral part of the sulking to which children often resort when challenged or shown any disapproval. A brooding, resentful silence can often result in a despairing parent relenting from some restriction or requirement placed upon a child, and forcing its eventual withdrawal – often with an apology and a bribe to 'make things better again'! This is, as we saw above, one of the many variants of the power game, the exertion of one person's will against another's. In this case, 'winning' is the pleasure of seeing the other person lose.

The game plan

The way in which we first become aware of a game being played is our regular experience of 'losing'. No matter what we do, or how we respond, we usually end up feeling the same: defeated. Having said that, you are now perhaps becoming aware of the games being played by someone close to you. If there is anything about which you are continually asking yourself, 'Why does this always happen to me?' then consider the following:

1. What is it that continually happens to you?
2. How does it begin?
3. In what context does this event take place? (groups, same sex or opposite sex individual relationships, parents?)
4. What happens next?
5. How does it always end up?
6. How do you feel at the end?
7. What conclusions do you arrive at as a result of this encounter?

This is the structure of what transactional analysts call *the game plan*. There is an inbuilt, logical structure about games and the way they progress to their conclusion in the payoff. One of the conclusions the woman mentioned above might arrive at is, 'These men are all wind and piss. Freeze them out for a while, and they'll come crawling back for forgiveness!' Or, 'I'll get you, you bastard, for daring to complain to me about my behaviour; I'll make you sorry you ever raised it!' These conclusions might not even be recognized consciously, but they are operating under the surface somewhere, and destroying the joy and spontaneity (not to mention honesty and love) the relationship needs. Let us watch two expert game-players in action; be aware of how the element of blaming gets expressed.

Case history: the games of Philippa and John

Philippa is invited to a Christmas party, where she enjoys a mild flirtation with John. Philippa sends out signals that she is available and interested, and enjoying John's pursuit. She acts coquettishly and, frankly, both she and John enjoy the game of pursuit and being pursued. She even agrees to him seeing her home after the party. When he tries to take things a stage further, by attempting to kiss Philippa goodnight, she turns on him, slaps his face hard, and asks what kind of woman he thinks she is! Exit John, in total disarray and perplexity.

Most of us can spot a game when we see one, but what is actually going on here, beneath the surface?

Philippa is acting the role of 'prick-tease', or what Berne called 'rapo', whereby she can indulge her coquettish fantasies and enjoy the pursuit and attention of John, while *at the same time* convincing herself that she is not that kind of woman at all, that nothing was ever further from her mind, that John (like all men, of course) is just out for one thing, and that she is in fact a good little girl at heart, just as Mummy taught her to be!

She has kept all her boundaries of morality intact, *and* enjoyed letting out that bit of herself which she dare only acknowledge in fantasy (and drink). The payoffs include:

- the maintenance of her self-image as pure and unsullied
- the enjoyment of being pursued by a man, reinforcing both her need to feel wanted and also her power to attract a man when she wants to
- seeing John discomfited and embarrassed
- the reinforcement of her concept of men as predatory animals
- she *really is* a good little girl.

Philippa could have a field day when she next met up with her girlfriends. 'You'll never imagine what that John tried on me after the party. . . .' Entirely innocent (in her own view) she can now lay all the blame for what happened on John. 'Nothing was further from my mind (of course) . . . men like John ought to be locked up. Innocent girls are not safe with men like him around the place. . . .' Philippa is enjoying the payoffs from this encounter, but her natural sensuality will not be gratified for long by a mere repetition of the Christmas party saga; it will seek out other opportunities for playing the game of 'rapo' with another dupe who will fall for that kind of game. Philippa comes out of such encounters with her conviction about her unsullied purity intact, and with her beliefs in the voracity of men reinforced. Should she ever have doubts about these twin platforms of her personal credo, she can always prove them once again at the next office party. . . !

But, I hear you object, 'What about John? Could he have been playing games too?' Indeed he could – and was!

If we look at John a little more closely, we discover that he never actually makes it with a girl. His history of relationships with women are, in fact, a disaster. Not that he is unattractive or has BO or anything like that. What John does not fully realize is that he is rather afraid of women; he is 'all talk and no action'. He too fantasizes about a deep, fully sexual, relationship with a woman like Philippa, but he would be scared out of his mind should she ever respond. Unconsciously, he therefore picks out women *who will reject him* before the 'great encounter' ever gets off the ground – or on the bed! John is playing the age-old game of 'Kick Me!'

This takes us back to younger days (childhood, again, is the source of many games) when we would pin a note saying 'Kick Me' on the jacket of someone at school. They would end up being kicked, not knowing what they had done to attract all this hostile reaction. (A refinement is when we pin another note saying, 'please don't kick me!' – a prohibition that is all but irresistible!)

But what is the payoff for John? He ends up feeling hurt and rejected: *precisely!* His advantages include:

- his credo is reinforced, that no matter how hard he tries, he will always end up being rejected
- he can abandon responsibility for what happened and place it squarely upon Philippa ('It was all her fault!')
- by playing 'Kick Me', John does not have to face up to the possibility of seeking meaningful, adult intimacy
- when John is in the bar with the other fellows, he can gain attention by dragging Philippa down, and use her 'awful behaviour' to consolidate his view of, 'That's women for you!'

• John never has to risk long-term relationships

So both John and Philippa could take part in a familiar version of the blaming game. While both protest their innocence, they are in fact receiving advantages from their different defensive stratagems. More importantly, neither of them has to relinquish their firmly held belief that the outcome was 'all the fault' of someone else. John could go on with his deficient view of women ('That's women for you!') and Philippa could continue with her conviction of the voracity of men ('That's men for you!'). This way, *nothing has to change*, the greatest advantage of all!

It is out of such painstaking analysis of the games people play that their fundamental, though unconscious needs are revealed. What might such needs look like, and where do they come from?

The fundamental needs of the game-player

Where does the drive come from that fuels the playing of such games as those of John and Philippa? People like these do not just indulge in games for the fun of it. The impetus is found in unconscious factors that have been entirely forgotten, and which at first might be thought of as utterly irrelevant. 'But I don't need to humiliate men!' Philippa could protest. Yet this is precisely what she *is* doing; even though it may be hard to find, nevertheless there is a reason behind such behaviour. 'But I don't need to be kicked by women!' John might protest. Yet, since this is exactly what is continually happening to him, some concealed principle is in operation. Behaviour such as Philippa's and John's does not 'just happen'.

Pay offs are sought after to meet hidden needs; they serve the purpose of reinforcing the twisted view of reality to which both these people, and thousands like them, were subjected in their infancy and childhood. The fact that they do not know such fundamental needs exist within them only serves to make them all the more dangerous.

Take Philippa first. It is very often the case, when women play 'Rapo', that there is some inner conflict concerning their own sexuality. Instead of this being expressed in joyful celebration, it has to come out in sneaky, underhand ways which give no lasting satisfaction. Guilt is never far away, and if we could know more about Philippa's own upbringing the seeds of her present problem would be revealed.

Similarly, John is also engineering his contacts with women so that his child, rather than his adult, needs are getting met. How come he needs to feel rejected, that women cannot be trusted, and that he cannot sustain a rewarding, adult, intimate relationship with a woman? Again, the answers lie somewhere deep in his personal history. Just because we do not know them does not make them any the less influential upon his life. We have seen the immediate advantages of his gamesmanship, and there are doubtless fundamental needs, or what we may call neurotic needs, which his game of 'Kick Me!' is meeting.

We only indulge in games when there do not seem to be any alternative ways of gaining some satisfaction. Anything is better than nothing. On the face of it, we find it hard to understand how anyone could indulge in game-playing which gives *negative* results, as in the game of 'Kick Me!' It may look like utter folly to pursue a game which has as its payoff a 'victim' or 'underdog' outcome, yet as we have seen there is more to playing games than first meets the eye. People who play games that inevitably lead to a result that includes being put down, or ending up as a 'loser', never have to take responsibility for anything. There *are* rewards for being weak, incapable and a failure. And some people have deeply ingrained investment in these rewards which is why so many of them are resistant to therapy and to the onslaught of well-meaning helpers who try to 'cure' them.

A further investment in playing games is found in the payoff of blaming our parents or our background. So we painfully uncover our childhood experiences, and discover that our parents were bastards, that we were damaged psychologically and that they have adversely affected our ability to think well of ourselves and live a fulfilling life. So what? We can now play the age-old game of 'Wooden Leg' – 'Well, what do you expect of a person with parents like mine?' or 'With parents like mine you expect me to be perfect?' One of its major payoffs is that we can avoid any responsibility for our lives. We play the blaming game, 'It's all their fault.' If the roots of the games played by Philippa and John were to be found in their childhood, they could add 'Wooden Leg' to their games of 'Rapo' and 'Kick Me'. As we shall see in Chapter 6, we need to give up blaming our parents or our past in order to mature and live game-free lives, and to abandon our need to fail.

The need to fail

Case history: Dominique

Dominique came to see me complaining of depression, about her husband's lack of attention to her, the untidiness of her two children, and the general state of chaos in her home. 'The place is a tip!' she would tell me. 'How do you feel?' I asked her. 'An utter failure!' she replied.

Here was an attractive woman, with a keen mind (she was a graduate in mathematics) feeling like a failure. She was sure therapy could not help her, since (being a failure) she was clearly beyond help. Her doctor told her she was heading for the local psychiatric ward, a thought that naturally filled her with horror. One day I asked her the sixty-four thousand dollar question: 'Why do you *need* to be a failure?' She looked at me intently, and said with emphasis: 'Only when people can see I'm a failure will they hear me!' 'Hear what?' I asked. 'I want them to hear that I need esteem even when I'm a failure!' We'd hit the payoff.

Dominique had an investment in failure. Saying she was attractive or gifted was totally dismissed. What she was actually depressed about was that her stratagems were not working! No-one took her 'failure game' seriously, so she had to allow the home to become a tip before they would believe her. She nearly went mad when the children started to clean the home since she had invested a lot of energy in letting it fall into chaos! The fundamental need of which, until then, she was herself hardly conscious, was that she wanted to be loved for being herself. She wanted to be loved, unlovable as she felt herself to be. Until other people around her noted her failure, she would get deeper and deeper into depression; it was a kind of desperate fight to the death.

In a world which is achievement-conscious, success-oriented, and rewarding only winners, it is hardly believable that anyone in their right mind (as Dominique clearly was) could actually court failure. But until this is understood and conveyed sympathetically to her, she will continue her downward spiral. Thus games, even with negative results, have a purpose in the human scheme of things. Such negative results meet some fundamental need within the total being of that person and that is why they prove so resistant to help. The unaware helper is in fact trying to take away a *solution* however much the person might protest that their way of behaving is actually a problem! It has certain problematic results, but they are worth experiencing for the greater gain that they unconsciously seek.

Dominique was, at the unconscious level, playing the Wooden Leg game: 'What do you expect of a woman with a house/husband/family like mine? What do you expect of a woman who is an utter failure?' What she did not know, until later, was that she was setting herself up to be a failure, while all the time complaining in such a way as to make her problems appear to be the results of some mysterious force of fate or destiny.

We are all part of the gaming process

This, then, is the gaming process in action. We have seen how it works out in the experiences of Philippa, John and Dominique. The chances are that as you have been reading their case histories you have had an uncomfortable feeling that you may have met these people before! Be sure of this: someone around you, right now, is playing games. Maybe even you?

This is not the same as saying that you, and those around you, are out-and-out liars. Gamesmanship can become such a natural part of our lives that we are not even conscious of a game going on. We do not consciously set out to deceive other people, put them (or ourselves) down, humiliate others (or ourselves). What we do know is that, time and time again, we end up feeling hurt, or hurting others, and we sometimes cannot even understand our own actions.

We say, 'But I love her, so why would I want to hurt her?' The only thing we know is that your desire to hurt her is stronger than your desire to love her. However things end up, there is a need for them to end up that way. Consciously, this puzzles us; subconsciously, there are strong emotional needs being met, and until they are raised to the level of consciousness, the game will go on, and people will go on being hurt.

The gaming process is a universal disease; we are all victims. We are all involved to some extent, however much we plead purity of thought and motive.

As a therapist, I know the damage that game-playing causes to thousands of people. I share some of their pain daily. It is out of a conscious desire to reduce the sum of human pain that I write this.

As a human being, I know the pain of uncovering my own game plans, and the shock and disbelief I encountered when they were discovered. I was not the kind, altruistic, Christian person I thought I was. My kindness, altruism and faith were all contaminated by hidden motives that were anything but kind, caring and Christian. The trick I was playing was that I wanted to be unkind and uncaring while at the same time appearing to be kind and caring!

While giving clear signals that I wished to be loved, I made sure I kept my distance so that the love could not be received. While consciously desiring intimacy, I always managed to arrange things so that intimacy was avoided. I could then entertain the fantasy that I lived in a world of hard, uncaring, unapproachable people. Why are there no warm, nurturing and inviting people around in my world, I wondered.

What was my unconscious game plan? Deeply buried within me was the conviction that no one would ever give me a second look! I was born with a colossal inferiority complex. So rather than risk the rejection that would almost certainly be inflicted on me by others if I ever dared to get close to them, I stage-managed events so that such closeness could be avoided. My inner weakness and worthlessness could remain hidden. That was *my* payoff – all the time living with the fantasy that my loneliness and isolation was all the fault of a world filled with uncaring, unloving people! The game plan involved massive concealment.

Over a long period of time in therapy and therapeutic groups, I slowly uncovered all this buried material. I discovered the origins of my feelings of inferiority, and the good self that lay beneath them. This entailed changing my inferior, worthless, frightened script for a more adult appreciation of myself. I learned how to love myself and found that self-acceptance led to a greater appreciation of others and my ability to get close enough to them to love them too.

I was no longer scared of intimacy. I could both love more freely, and allow myself to be loved openly and passionately. I decided to be an adult in a grown-up world, risking the pain of being honest and open, which I found far preferable to the pain of being dishonest and concealed behind vast outdated defences.

What is more, I had discovered the inner dynamics of a sinister form of activity, which robbed me of my self-respect and at the same time distanced me from others: the blaming game.

6

How to Quit
the Blaming Game

We have seen how the blaming game is often a cover-up, a defence against having to take responsibility for what we do in our lives. Only when we appreciate the full implications of blaming other people for our own mistakes, will we be in a position to think about quitting the blaming game for good. Some of these implications have been spelt out in the previous chapters, but for the sake of clarity, I will summarize them here:

1. Blaming others for what we do, or fail to do, is an attempt to get them to take responsibility.
2. Blaming others is an attempt to escape having to admit our own mistakes; better to put the blame on someone else.
3. Blaming other people justifies our own continuing resentment; while we hold them responsible for our feelings, we do not have to change.
4. Fear of taking responsibility lies at the heart of the blaming game.
5. If we can place the blame for our own actions on someone else, we make them responsible for putting things right again.
6. If blaming others arises out of the fear of accepting responsibility for what *we* have done, then blaming ourselves arises out of the unwillingness to allow other people to take responsibility for what *they* have done.
7. To blame other people involves a payoff, usually the maintenance of our own supposed innocence.
8. Fear of punishment for the wrongs we do motivates the blaming of other people.
9. 'It's always your fault!' and 'It's always my fault!' are both lies; no one person can be in the wrong all the time.
10. If I blame other people for my mistakes, I am evoking a

sense of guilt within them, and this gives me a sense of power over them.

11. Blaming others ensures that I can avoid looking into myself too closely, and thus I can avoid any changes to my own behaviour.

12. When I blame other people for what I have done, or failed to do, I vote for staying stuck in my own blindness.

13. Staying stuck in my own blindness is better than becoming aware of who I really am, because otherwise I might have to change.

14. When I continue to blame myself for surviving some disaster I am preferring the pain of depression to a conscious recognition of my own limitations.

Blaming, therefore, is merely the tip of a very large and complicated psychological iceberg. You cannot quit the blaming game until and unless these underlying causes are uncovered and explored.

Keywords in the blaming game

Some important 'keywords' are contained in the above summary:

responsibility – avoidance – fear – guilt and innocence – punishment – awareness

These keywords supply us with a psychological map for this necessary exploration; they help us to find a way through to a more healthy way of being and behaving in our world.

For me, the starting point is that of awareness.

Awareness

Most of us can remember what it feels like to be blamed for something that we have not done. Such feelings are a mixture of anger, humiliation, unfairness and resentment. The downward spiral that blaming initiates always ends up with someone getting hurt, but we need to take a hard look at ourselves before we start polishing up our own personal haloes! Through the activity of placing upon others responsibility for our own mistakes we are voting for a further fragmentation of the world of human relationships, and diminishing the sum of human happiness. We cannot morally escape the consequences of our actions.

Thankfully, there are enough people in this world who refuse to take the responsibility we try to lay upon them wrongfully. They will refuse to play the game, and their refusal challenges us to increase our awareness of what we are trying to do, even if it is merely out of a longstanding habit. Many people will simply deny responsibility, and in so many words tell us to get lost. The more understanding among us might reply, when wrongfully blamed, 'Why are you trying to lay the blame for your own wrongs on me?' This avoids the arid, 'Yes, you are!', 'No, I'm not!' encounter. We can draw other people's attention to what is actually going on, and to how we feel about what is going on. Another adult reply to the blaming game would be, 'Are you aware that every time you make a mistake, you end up blaming me for it?' Again, this is a consciousness-raising kind of question that invites the perpetrator to become aware of what he/she is doing. When the blaming game is going on between intimates, the need for this kind of question becomes even more necessary. The wrongly accused can respond with, 'I'm getting very angry when you try to make me responsible for your actions!' We do not have to sit idly by and simply take the blame when it is dumped on us. We do not have to 'take the rap'.

No one is going to quit the blaming game until they become aware of what they are doing, and of its effect upon people who care about them. I was attending an enrolment evening for a course I was teaching and two young women came up to enrol. 'She talked me into it!' said one about the other. It appeared an innocent, even jocular remark, but the sinister seeds of the blaming game were apparent. I responded, 'No she didn't! You agreed to be talked into it. The decision is yours!' But if the

course had turned out to be a waste of time and money who will
end up taking the blame? You've guessed it: her friend.

So we begin to quit the blaming game when we become *aware*
of what we are doing, and that means that we need to have some
people around us who are prepared to take the risk of being
honest with us. 'Are you aware. . . ?', is a good way to begin to
do this with people who show *no* awareness of what they are
doing. 'Are you aware that it was you who chose to go on that
course?' is an appropriately adult question to ask our friend.
Awareness is a movement from the unknown to the known, from
not recognizing what we are doing to recognizing our own
choices. It is an important step from blindness to sight. For most
people who play the blaming game are simply not aware of what
they are doing. They have become so used to covering up their
mistakes by denying that they had anything to do with them, that
blaming has become a way of life for them. Since they cannot
(ever) be in the wrong, others must take the blame. Unfortu-
nately, there are almost as many 'can-carriers' as there are
people who want others to carry them, and they too need to
become aware of what they are doing, and why.

The 'can-carriers' of this world are those who compulsively
take responsibility for everything that goes wrong in a relationship. They simply will not allow anyone else to take their rightful
responsibility. They (mistakenly) perceive their role in the
marriage or relationship as the family 'dustbin', the carrier of the
family's rubbish. Many people who eventually need counselling
or psychotherapy for personality disorders present this kind of
symptom among their catalogue of ills. Psychologist Dorothy
Rowe comments:

> There isn't anything that can happen in the entire universe that
> they cannot see themselves as responsible for and feel guilty
> about. Usually they confine their responsibility to their family
> and their job. They are entirely responsible for the happiness
> of their spouse, children, parents, brothers and sisters,
> grandparents and, if they are so minded, to the entire range of
> their cousins and in-laws. None of these relatives is capable of

being responsible for himself or herself. If my client is working then no matter what his job is, he is responsible for the welfare of the entire organization, no matter if it is an international business or a vast government department. My client sees himself as responsible for everything, and when he sees himself as failing in his responsibility he says, 'I feel so guilty. I should take Mum and Dad out more often/I should have made sure my son worked harder for his university exams/I should set an example to the others in the office/If I had given my sister more help her husband wouldn't have left her/It's my fault if any of my pupils fail their A levels' and so on.

(*Depression: The Way Out of Your Prison*, Routledge 1983, p. 135)

People like this remind me of a description once made by my mentor Dr Frank Lake: 'Some people,' he said, 'appear to be suffering from a hardening of the "oughteries"!'

It often turns out that someone in the family has elected someone else as the family 'black sheep' or 'scapegoat' (see Chapter 2). Think of all the sentences you have heard (or spoken!) that begin with, 'If it weren't for you. . . .' This is a prime move in the blaming game, intended to make another person responsible for all the family woes. Perhaps for a while, this role as family dustbin was resisted, but finally the odds stacked against them were too hard to cope with, and they caved in and accepted as true the 'badness' placed upon them.

Both the compulsive blamer and the compulsive recipient of blame need awareness. Here are a few more statements designed to increase awareness in the unaware.

- I refuse to accept the blame for. . . .
- You made that decision, not me!
- That's not my responsibility; it's yours!
- Why do you find it so hard to take the blame yourself?
- I didn't make you . . . you chose to!
- Take responsibility for your own choices!

- I really resent it when you try to make me responsible for your mistakes!
- Are you aware that the decision to enrol for that course was yours, not mine?
- I'm not going to allow you to treat me like a scapegoat any longer!
- I'm fed up being treated like the family dustbin!
- I don't accept that I alone am responsible for your misery!
- Why do you always have to accept the blame for everything that goes wrong in our marriage?

Guilt and innocence

Here are two more keywords in the vocabulary of the blaming game. They are never very far below the surface of what is going on. Each of those words – or the issues behind them – has a history in our family upbringing, and we do well to recall what it was. What happened to the guilty ones and the innocent ones, and in which group did we usually find ourselves? 'Feeling guilty' is an uncomfortable experience at the best of times. We spend a lot of energy, therefore, in trying to escape such feelings. One ploy is to transfer the nasty feeling on to someone else; let them carry the can. Children are apparently natural players of the blaming game, and most of us have either had, or heard of, the experience whereby someone got blamed for something they did not do, only they could not prove it and were punished wrongly. This breeds another problem, namely revenge, and we are then already on the slippery spiral of finding ways to get our own back on the real culprits. We then protest our innocence, and become the blamer ourselves, and round and round the game goes, like a contagious disease in the home. Thousands of brothers and sisters have been set against each other, and whole families divided by people blaming someone else for their own misdeeds.

The way through this vast desert of pain and unhappiness is to come clean about what we have done. To admit to what we have done wrong is a courageous thing to do, but the lengths to which we will go to avoid this admission is staggering. We want to avoid being told off, but if we deny our culpability we have to live with that lie. That does far more damage to our personality than owning up to it in the first place. Integrity comes into this issue, being able to live with ourselves, but a lifetime of passing the buck onto someone else dulls our consciences and we end up believing in our own lies. We are then the 'innocent'-guilty ones. We need to take a long, hard look at our own methods of escape and ask ourselves some searching questions about them. 'What was happening in me when I told that lie? What was I afraid of when I passed the buck to that other driver?' (Was it losing my no claims bonus, perhaps?) So what is more damaging: losing my no claims bonus or my self-respect?

The other issue here in the admission of actual guilt is that the event is then able to be put in the past and forgotten. The alternative, of hiding and denying it, is to prolong it. It is like carrying an enormous debt that we can never pay back, because we are denying we owe it in the first place! The taxman receives thousands of pounds every year from people with guilty consciences who find they can no longer live with the deceit of having defrauded the government out of rightful revenue. A good conscience is far better than a bad one, and is much more beneficial to your health.

Some things we do, however, can never be put right. Restitution can be made in the case of money, but what happens in the case of loss of life? What can we say to the hit-and-run driver who kills an innocent child on the road? Or to the drunk driver who mows down a row of people on a pedestrian crossing? In other words, how can that person quit the blaming game of self-accusation? Such hard cases are often the subject of long-term counselling and psychotherapy and these might be the best agencies to deal with them. As a psychotherapist, I can only share with you my own approach to those who feel they can no longer go on living with the enormity of their guilt and seek some resolution.

Case history: Joy

Joy came to see me concerning her recurring bouts of

depression. She had tried antidepressants, but her GP wisely thought that therapy might do her far more good and recommended her to see me. It eventually emerged that she was nursing a tremendous guilty conscience concerning an abortion that had taken place some months previously. She was obsessed with the thought of having taken a life; this presented her with a moral problem never previously encountered (she had no religious affiliations). She told her story amid much crying, and I gently encouraged her to go through the decision-making process in as much detail as she could remember. What, of course, she had never done was to grieve over the loss of her baby; her guilt had got in the way of that. That grief was entirely appropriate. I asked her to join me on the floor of my consulting room, and I arranged a small cushion to represent the baby. I asked her to imagine that there was a very tiny fetus on the cushion, her potential child, and invited her to talk to it.

Joy began, naturally, rather self-consciously but with minimal prompting from me, she began to tell the 'baby' how it came about that she decided to terminate her pregnancy. A wider picture emerged. There was pressure from her parents and from her boyfriend to have an abortion. There was her career to think of. At each confession, I asked Joy to direct this to 'her baby'. In psychological terms, it was impossible for her to say goodbye to her baby until she had said, 'hello', and in this imaginary/actual dialogue she was beginning to form the necessary relationship prior to saying goodbye to the child. The time came for her to say goodbye; she hugged the cushion to her and told the child how sorry she was to have taken its life. She had felt trapped between the need to preserve life, and the needs of her parents, her boyfriend and her own career too. She finally accepted responsibility for the decision she had made, and this led me into the invitation to find a way in which she could forgive herself. She asked the 'baby' to forgive her, and she imagined the 'baby' doing this. She was able to receive its forgiveness, and eventually to forgive herself. 'We don't always get things right in life all the time,' I told her, 'it is part of our own brokenness.' Having admitted her feelings of guilt, and her need of forgiveness – not least by herself – she was at least more able to live a reasonably happy life in the future. One mistake need not necessarily lead to two. Since, in this case, nothing could be done to reverse the original event, she might at least be able to seek future happiness free from a crippling sense of guilt.

Guilt need not be a life sentence. As Joy came to forgive herself, she became less depressed. She was more able to become an agent of healing to others after she herself was healed within. She had completed the 'unfinished business' of the pregnancy, which no amount of denial or avoidance – or false comfort from parents and well-meaning others – could ever do. A small part of this world's pain was at least healed.

In dealing with actual guilt, it is never wise to try to get the person to bury it deeper within themselves. This merely makes matters worse. Rather the therapeutic requirement is to enable the person openly and honestly to explore their actions and to accept fully their responsibility – or share of responsibility – for what took place. The need then is to seek self-forgiveness, which is really a process of letting it go. In the paradoxical way in which therapy works, you can only let past guilt go once you have accepted it.

'That's all very well,' I hear someone say, 'but isn't all this merely special pleading?' After all, it could be said, 'guilt is guilt!' I fully realize that there are many voices which would be raised in protest to what I have said above. There will always be those who find forgiveness hard, especially for themselves. 'I'll never forgive myself!' is often said, but this implies a self-imposed life sentence of misery. There is no need – either morally or practically – for us to live out the rest of our lives in this state of regret and mental self-flagellation. Two wrongs never do make a right. There is far more misery in this world in the hearts and minds of those tortured with guilt than we could ever imagine. This is not a case of wanting a 'forgive-and-forget' policy: some things we do or fail to do we can never forget. But we can stop blaming ourselves by using self-forgiveness, recognizing that our own stupidity or sinfulness is but a *part* of who we are, not the whole. Being human, we are prone to error; being imperfect beings, we are liable to do imperfect things at times. The purpose of guilt is not intended to act as a permanent judgement hanging over our heads; rather, it is to be found in its goading us towards a recognition of our true responsibility for our deeds, to remedy what we can, and ultimately to work towards a way of forgiving ourselves.

Punishment

In learning how to quit the blaming game, we need to find out for ourselves what are our own attitudes towards punishment. Like other keywords, we do not come to this word neutrally. We bring with us our own experiences of being punished, especially our childhood memories, and our attitudes towards others who, in our opinion at least, deserve to be punished. Opinions will differ, ranging from the utterly squeamish who 'couldn't hurt a fly', to the 'hang-em, bring-back-the-birch' brigade. This is part of the wider social argument that has been going on for generations. What is the purpose of punishment? Is it supposed to be remedial and educative, in which case bringing back the death penalty hardly fits the bill; or is it – as the name implies – to be thought of as punitive, that is the payment of a penalty. This is not necessarily vindictive or sadistic. Penalties belong to a world of rules and law. In sport, for example, certain activities and behaviour incur penalties. They are there not in order to spoil the fun, but to ensure that the fun remains. Without some sort of law and order society disintegrates. With children, we are both taught and probably teach that a breach of the 'rules' will incur penalties; that is a form of punishment. This is a just way of ensuring that the family rules are kept, and while they may not always be morally just, nevertheless that is how the family operates. *Penalties, therefore, establish boundaries*, and we transgress (literally 'go across') them at our peril. Like double yellow lines, we know what they mean and if we chance parking our car on them, and consequently receive a fine, we can hardly complain.

In both families (the microcosm) and society (the macrocosm), therefore, boundaries are established in order to maintain a working relationship with those around us. They are what makes a civilization practical, and at least reasonably safe. Of course, most of us want it all our own way: we want the rules (for when others break them we are the first to cry, 'Foul!'), but we also want to break the rules and not have to pay the penalty. How many car drivers complain at the speed of traffic along their road, when they themselves ignore the speed limit along roads where other people live? This is just a small illustration of the double-standards we operate in our attitudes towards culpability. 'Serves him right,' we say, when some prominent personality gets a jail sentence for tax evasion; at the same time, however, we turn a blind eye to our own fiddles. And when these get rumbled, we scream 'unfair!' We turn on the 'what-about-so-and-so?' record in order to excuse ourselves; we believe ourselves to be minnows in an ocean of sharks. And so we might be. But both minnows and sharks are subject to the same rules, and it is a mark of maturity when we can acknowledge our wrongdoing without excusing ourselves.

Alfred Adler, the noted psychologist, saw clearly into the attitude of neurotic people who aggressively fix the blame for their failures on to other people or circumstances. Here is his catalogue of excuses:

It is the fault of my parents, my fate; because I am the youngest, was born too late; because I am a Cinderella; because I am perhaps not the child of these parents, of this father, of this mother; because I am too small, too weak, have too small a head, am too homely; because I have a speech defect, a hearing defect, am cross-eyed, nearsighted; because I have misshaped genitals, because I am not manly, because I am a girl; because I am by nature bad, stupid, awkward; because I have masturbated; because I am too sensuous, too covetous, and naturally perverted; because I submit easily, am too dependent and obedient; because I cry easily, am easily moved; because I am a criminal, a thief, an incendiary, and could murder someone; my ancestry, my education, my circumcision are to blame; because I have a long nose, too much hair; because I am a cripple; because I have been pampered, and because I have been discriminated against.

(quoted in C. R. Snyder et al. *Excuses*, John Wiley & Sons 1983, p. 205).

In order to avoid punishment we turn to blaming. I found this out recently in an episode where my six-year-old daughter taught me an uncomfortable lesson.

Katie was watching a video just before her bedtime, and she asked Mummy to watch it with her. This was their time together. I suddenly rushed into the room and asked my wife to take a look at something I'd written. As she did so, Katie took the paper from Jan. Ignoring Katie's signal, we both chided her for her bad manners, whereupon she stomped out of the room up to bed. It was only later that my wife and I realized what we had done. One of our home rules is 'Don't interrupt!' and here I was, unthinkingly, interrupting her time with her mother. The fault was entirely mine, not Katie's. I went up to her bedroom and said I was sorry for interrupting her time with Mummy, and that I had made a mistake. I told her I was wrong to expect one kind of behaviour from her, and another from myself. I promised to try to be more thoughtful in the future. I hope she understood. It would have been so easy to punish Katie for being moody and irritable, and then to forget it. But I owed that apology, as much for my benefit (to keep me truthful) as for hers (to create a model of truthfulness). Although my first instinct in this episode was to punish Katie for her rudeness, by seeing that it was not her but me who was at fault, I could admit the blame and ask for her forgiveness. This may seem a small event to you, but I can only say that, not so long ago, wild horses would not have wrung that apology from me!

We quit the blaming game when we can abandon our need to punish others for our mistakes. Neither do we have to make the opposite error of punishing ourselves for having made one. The best we can hope for is, in the title of Bruno Bettelheim's book, to be a '*Good Enough Parent*' (Pan 1987).

Avoidance

So what was it that, years ago, I would have wanted to avoid? I suppose it was simply admitting that I had made a mistake, that I was wrong, that it was my fault, not Katie's. Most of us have our avoidance techniques pretty well perfected by the time we reach adult life.

Our behavioural avoidance techniques are part of our natural inheritance. Some of these have to do with our inbuilt, self-protective, survival instincts. This is part of our evolutionary legacy. We would not be here if it were not for them! Then there is our highly sophisticated immune system, which resists the invasion of foreign bodies (even those transplants that might save our lives), and is part of an avoidance system that we inherit as being human. However, there is a parallel, psychological avoidance system at work within us which has nothing at all to do with our physical survival. It does have something to do with the avoidance of pain, however, but we confuse this psychological pain with life-threatening pain, and it is here that we make our mistake. Admitting I am wrong does not threaten my life! Confessing to a fault may threaten my *reputation* – especially if I have been busily building up an image of perfection – but it will not endanger my *existence*. Accepting appropriate blame may affect my wellbeing, but not my sense of being. This is a crucial distinction, and failure to make it lies at the heart of many of our avoidance techniques. We mistake accepting liability for losing life.

No wonder, then, we try to avoid potentially painful situations. If our inherited genetic impulses of self-preservation don't make us run from them, our painstaking efforts at projecting a 'goody-goody' image will.

There is no quitting the blaming game until we practise the attribution and acceptance of real blame, rather than the avoidance of blame.

Here are a few suggested linguistic statements that we might profitably learn. We may choke on some of them at first, but with practice they'll come more naturally:

- 'I'm sorry, I'm really sorry.'

Here are the dreaded words of apology, which many of us find so hard to utter. Others, of course, can hardly stop themselves from saying them! They are the 'walking apologies' of this world. It's interesting to find that, when using these words, other people may want to take the responsibility away from us. 'Oh, no. It was all my fault!' they say. Such people are trying to misappropriate your responsibility and make it their own. Resist them!

- 'That was my fault.'

This simple admission of error is very hard for some people to utter. Have you noticed that some people push you hard to take responsibility for what you have done, only to be possessed by an equally strong desire to talk you out of doing so once you admit your fault? Once we can function in our 'adult' mode, as opposed to our conditioned 'child' response, we are able to admit to our wrongdoing without fear of reprisals.

- 'I apologize.'

An apology is a statement of regret for a fault you have done or contributed to. This means that we need only apologize for that part of the event, or circumstances, that we are responsible for. As we noted on the spectrum of blame, we need to recognize where we are on the scale of responsibility and to be ready to acknowledge our part in the present state of affairs. This response is different from the following one.

- 'I accept full responsibility for that.'

Here is a confession of total responsibility for the state of affairs confronting us. If I run into the back of your car because I am not looking, I could play games about your car being in the wrong place at the wrong time, but this is futile. I can admit total liability, and seek to compensate you for the damage done. Whatever we take responsibility for, we are to that extent liable to put things right again, as far as is possible. If I do not share with you my needs, I cannot reasonably make you responsible for failing to meet my needs. But this is what happens in many relationships.

● 'I made a mistake.'

For those of us brought up on a diet of perfectionism and conditional love, this is going to be a hard thing to confess. So often we confuse loss of face with loss of being. To own up to a mistake might be thought of as threatening our being, instead of our reputaton. But such admissions are not signs of weakness, which is what we fear others will think; rather they are signs of strength, that we are big enough to own up to our mistakes and not be tempted to make others responsible for them. We grow when we can own our mistakes instead of blaming others.

● 'I admit that what you say is true. I lied.'

Lying is one of our most familiar avoidance techniques. Today, we are in danger of using lies even about our lying, as in the recently used phrase, 'economical with the truth'! It may sound witty, but it is a cover-up. Someone else usually has to carry the blame for our lies, and our integrity will suffer as long as we continue to dissemble with truth.

● 'It was me. I did it.'

This statement is so unusual that it will probably be greeted by gasps of astonishment. We tend to admire direct confessions of responsibility in others, while finding them difficult to make for ourselves. This approach ensures that we don't get caught up in lies or blaming others. This direct admission means that we do not have to spend valuable energy denying the truth, and covering up our actions.

● 'You are not to blame.'

Only those who have been on the receiving end of this kind of exoneration know the relief that these words can bring. I was speaking to a man recently who had been involved in a widely publicized accident which resulted in the deaths of several people. At the inquest, some friends of one of the people who died in the accident came up and told him that they did not hold him to blame for what happened. He told me how relieved he felt by those words, and they were directly responsible for much of his later healing from this terrible event.

- 'Please forgive me.'

Needing the forgiveness of other people often places us in their power and control; they can either give or withhold. None of us really likes being beholden to other people, but there are occasions when we need to be forgiven by those whom we have wronged. We need to ask for their pardon to begin to mend the broken relationship, broken by our wrongdoing, spite or foolishness.

Forgiveness is not forgetting. Some of the wrongs we have done, or have had done to us by others, we can never forget, such is the measure of the pain or betrayal. Forgiveness is the ability and willingness to cease holding the wrong against others. It's like tearing up an IOU and refusing to make any further claims upon the person for the damage they have done to us. This is the importance of asking for others to forgive us for the wrong we have done. We are asking them to tear up our IOU and work towards mending the broken relationship without raking up the past. No one finds this easy, but it is possible, if we really want the relationship to get back on to a more friendly basis, to ask for forgiveness from those we have wronged.

- 'You're right to feel angry about what I've just done.'

This is a plain justification of the feelings of the other person. Anger usually makes us feel uncomfortable, whether it belongs to us or to other people. It is a very strong emotion, and some of us cannot handle it at all well. We may have come to associate anger with violence, even verbal violence, and we naturally try to avoid it. But anger is a very positive emotion if expressed

93

appropriately. Sam Keen quotes an entry in his own journal as he dialogues with his own anger:

ANGER: Did you ever consider how valuable I am to you?
SAM KEEN: In what ways?
ANGER: I keep you safe by making your full strength available to you in situations of danger. I help you to identify those enemies that threaten your well-being. I defend your boundaries of the physical, psychological, economic, and social space you need to survive. And, I might say, I add as much spice to life as your highly idealized love. I keep one person from being swallowed up by another and thus preserve the duality which is necessary for love. . . . If you can't fight, you can't love.

(*To a Dancing God*, Fontana 1971, p. 116)

What is it that prevents us from making such statements more regularly than we do? It is what actually gives rise to our avoidance techniques, feeds them, continues them: *the spectre of fear*.

Fear

Fear is one of our most basic and primitive drives. The origins of fear go back to the earliest stages of our evolutionary development, whereby fear protected us in actual or potential danger. (Indeed, the word 'fear' comes from an Old English word 'faer', meaning sudden calamity or danger.) Survival instincts prevail in all living things, that self-defensive mechanism which operates at all levels of being. Having carried this instinct with us for so long, we are reluctant to abandon it, even when it now operates *against* us.

But can we just abandon fear? Is this even possible or desirable? I'd like to tackle these questions by making an important distinction between a rational and an irrational fear. There are many things that we do well to fear: a fire in the home, road accidents, mugging on our streets. All these are potentially life-threatening situations, and we need our protection of fear to guard against them. The human organism has trained itself over millenia to do this, and we are not going to stop the force of evolution by an act of will. On the other hand, however, there are situations that are not life-threatening at all, but are covered by the irrational element in fear. It is, for instance, irrational fear that lies at the heart of most of the phobic personality disorders: agoraphobia, cancer phobia, school phobia, etc. These phobias arise from within us, not from our external circumstances, although they may get projected onto the world outside. It is within this sphere of irrational fear that our fear of accepting responsibility for our own actions arises. If we regard others as enemies, and any admission of guilt as signing our own death warrant, of course we will avoid blame. We will do more: we will lie in our teeth, commit perjury, twist the truth, and rather see others suffering (innocently) for what we have done, than admit that we are the guilty party, all because of an irrational fear of suffering.

The implications of this pattern of behaviour, however, go far beyond this. Having landed someone else in the mire for what we have done, we do not escape suffering. We know what we have done, and sometimes we do not feel good about it. Of course, there are some psychopathic personalities who can go round mugging old ladies without a twinge of conscience, but most of us who still retain an ounce of feeling will experience a guilty conscience, and feel bad about what we have done. So having avoided suffering through fear, we now experience suffering through guilt instead! Now we have another problem to deal with: what do we do with our feelings of guilt? Well, if we are British then in the time-honoured British way we will bury them, bottle them up, try to forget it ever happened, adopt a false 'devil-may-care' attitude, and try whistling in the dark. So far, so good. But there is another element that creeps in at this point.

Whenever we bury unacceptable feelings, or try to suppress a tender conscience, there are some inevitable consequences. First, we use up a vast amount of psychic energy keeping our guilty conscience quiet. While one part of us that knows we have done wrong and should admit it, another part of us, governed by fear, is pushing the other bit down, burying it at the bottom of our mental dustbin. This conflict is unceasing. Day and night, we have to use up energy keeping the lid on the dustbin, in case the unwelcome thoughts arise into our consciousness and disturb our phoney peace. Finally, we have licked it! No more awkward thoughts about what we did. It is all in the past now, so we think. It is over and forgotten. We may have forgotten 'it', but 'it' has not forgotten us. Those buried thoughts and feelings have been *buried alive*! More and more energy has to go into keeping up this uneasy truce with our conscience, and we finally discover that something is happening to us that we do not like.

We then find we are waking up in the morning as tired as when we went to bed. Our eight hours' sleep does nothing for us. We get no rest from sleep. We also find that life has become dull and uninteresting, an unending grind; nothing pleases us any more. There is no joy, no pleasure from anything; even food tastes like sawdust. We are short-tempered, have no patience with anyone. We feel 'down' all the time. And we do not know why. Finally, we cannot keep up the pretence any longer; something is the matter with us, and we fix an appointment to see the doctor. The doctor listens to us, and then says, 'You're depressed!'

The rule seems to be, then, *suppression leads to depression*. So in spite of our avoidance techniques in relation to fear and suffering, we end up suffering after all. We have not escaped! Rather, we are now in the prison of depression – and we have swallowed the key.

The way out of this prison – not surprisingly – is precisely the same way we got into it in the first place. Every single step of the way that led to our depression has to be retrod as we climb out. The identical issues that produced our depression have to be faced if ever we are to get out of it. All that we ran away from eventually has to be faced, and a more constructive method of dealing with those issues must be found if we are to progress out of our depression. Antidepressants are not the answer; they may help us for a while, give us strength to seek other forms of help, but they are merely temporary props. In the end, it is those 'other voices in other rooms' (to use Truman Capote's evocative phrase) to which we need to pay attention. What were we running away from in the first place? Why, suffering of course! And how do we feel now – months or years, and several bottles of antidepressants later? Why, still suffering, of course! What have we achieved? Nothing.

In *Psychology and Religion: West and East* (Princeton Univ. Press 1973, p. 75) Carl Jung summed all this up in the best one-liner I have ever found:

Neurosis is always a substitute for legitimate suffering.

Attempting to avoid the legitimate suffering of the admission of fear and guilt, we fall into the substitute suffering that we call depression. And since 'depression' is what we feel instead of feeling something else, it cannot be cured until we are prepared to deal with that important 'something else'. We pay dearly for avoiding the fear involved in the admission of blame. And the way out? The way out is the way of *responsibility*.

Responsibility

This is *the key* to quitting the blaming game. We need to learn, or – if we have forgotten – *re*learn, how to take appropriate responsibility for our own behaviour and actions. I say 'appropriate', for, as we have seen previously, there is an *in*appropriate way in which we can take responsibility.

So what is normal, appropriate, responsibility?

Normal responsibility arises out of the ability to respond to a situation appropriately: response-ability. While we all possess the capability of doing this, most of us are conditioned to avoid responsibility for the reasons mentioned earlier. *To accept responsibility we need to grow up, to mature.* These two realities go hand in hand. We need to grow up and out of our childhood ways of behaviour, and to become an adult. Adulthood has nothing to do with age; your birth certificate only tells you when you were born, not your age! You can still be acting like a spoilt child well into your forties and fifties, and beyond. Adulthood has to do with how mature you are; when your behaviour is appropriate to your age then you are becoming mature. The alternative to the blaming game is 'growing up'.

We quit the blaming game only when we mature.
If it is that simple, then why do we not do it? While there are many benefits from becoming a mature adult, there are also some disadvantages which we do well to bear in mind.

Hanging on to childhood has its advantages. In childhood there were plenty of other people around to look after us, and to take responsibility for our world when it went wrong. When we were ill, Mum would 'phone the doctor; when we were hard up, Dad would cough up extra pocket money. When there was difficult homework, older brother would help us out; when we did not turn up for a soccer match, someone would act as a substitute. And so on. The difficult truth is that, with advantages attaching to a childish view of the world, very few of us are willing to give them up. We hang on to them.

Case history: Annie

A GP rang me up one day. Would I see one of his patients who was suffering from a range of problems not immediately responding to medical treatment? 'Tell her to come and see me,' I said. 'Ah, that's the problem,' said the GP; 'she's got agoraphobia and can't get out of the house!' 'Then how do *you* see her?' I replied. 'Her mother brings her to the surgery.' I then arranged to see his patient at his surgery, since we knew she could manage to get that far. My first impression of Annie was that of a young girl. She appeared to me to be about fifteen, but the GP had told me that she was thirty-one. Her story was a sad and complicated one. A catalogue of woes were trundled out and the outcome was that she was incarcerated in her mother's home, with her mother doing everything for her.

In the strange way that therapists often operate, I started to convert her story (in my head) from a tragedy to an all-too-convenient *solution*. I began to reckon up all the *positive advantages* which this string of symptoms she complained of might have. Having a mother waiting on you hand and foot, and an arsenal of symptoms that were conveniently poised to prevent you from doing anything you did not wish to do seemed just too suspicious by far. Was her 'problem' a 'payoff' in disguise?

I took my courage (and what was left of my reputation) in both hands. I told Annie that if I had a list of symptoms like hers, with the *benefits* that attached to them, I would not give them up for all the tea in China! I would hang on to them for all I was worth, and would not let *anyone* take them away from me. I would resist all sources of help (inside, of course) while shouting 'victim', and 'help me!' She blew up. 'You don't think I enjoy being this way, do you?' I said that it could be one possibility! I told her that, while I heard the sadness she complained of, it might be a small price to pay for the payoff of being ill. Only when she decided to grow up and join the rest of the adults, and abandon her childish game, would she ever feel any better. The venom in her eyes and voice told me I had hit the button.

I never saw her again. She quit therapy.

In this case, there was an interesting postscript. Quite by chance, I met a woman who said to me, 'You won't remember me, but you used to see my daughter some years ago.' Of course, I had no idea to whom she was referring, and said so. 'It doesn't matter,' she replied, 'only I wanted to say to you that I don't know what it was you said to her on her last appointment but it has revolutionized her life. She has now left home, got a job and a boyfriend and is living a normal life again. I can't thank you enough!'

When I got home and looked up my records, I realized who I had been speaking to. She was Annie's mother. And what was this 'magic cure' I had come up with? *Responsibility*. What was it that the young woman had been so patently avoiding? *Responsibility*. What was it that revolutionized her life and gave her back her dignity, purpose and freedom? Me? No; *responsibility*.

Only when this young woman decided to quit her childhood with its convenient rewards did she change. I did not do it. She did. It was her decision. Somewhere along the path, she voted for growing up – and then reaped the benefits that were far more rewarding than those to which she previously clung with such childish tenacity.

The lesson seems to be: before you can take responsibility for your life, you have to risk letting something go. Before you can say 'hello' to adulthood you need to say 'goodbye' to childhood. *Taking* responsibility means *leaving* irresponsibility.

Only when you leave the world of excuses and avoidance techniques behind will you quit the blaming game.

Further Reading

Berne, Eric, *Games People Play*, Penguin 1964.

Gough, Tony, *Couples Arguing*, Darton, Longman and Todd 1987.

Gough, Tony, *Couples in Counselling*, Darton, Longman and Todd 1989.

Harris, Thomas, *I'm OK, You're OK*, Pan 1973.

Oden, Thomas C., *Game Free*, Harper & Row 1974.

Useful Addresses

The British Association for Counselling
37a Sheep Street,
RUGBY
Warwickshire, CV21 3BX
Telephone 0788–78328/9
(The BAC publishes a Directory every year of both counselling organisations and private counsellors and should be available in local libraries.)

RELATE (The National Marriage Guidance Council)
Head Office
Herbert Gray College
Little Church Street
RUGBY
Warwickshire, CV21 3AP
Telephone 0788–73241
(Consult your telephone directory for local offices.)

The Westminster Pastoral Foundation
23 Kensington Square
LONDON W8 5HN
Telephone 071–937 6956
(The WPF have counselling centres in many areas.)

Index